Jaime J. Such

D0337450

GOLDEN RETRIEVERS

Everything about Purchase, Care,
Nutrition, Breeding, Behavior and Training

With Color Photographs by Well-Known Photographers
and Drawings by Michele Earle-Bridges

Consulting Editor: Matthew M. Vriends, Ph.D.

BARRON'S

New York • London • Toronto • Sydney

Photo Credits
Eugene Butenas (LCA Photography): inside front cover;
page 17; page 36, top; page 63, top right and bottom;
page 64; inside back cover, top left.
Raymond D. Kopen: page 63, top left.
Wim van Vugt: cover; page 18; page 35; page 36,
bottom; page 53; page 54; back cover, top right and
bottom.

© Copyright 1987 by Barron's Educational Series, Inc.

All rights reserved.

No part of this book may be reproduced in any form by
photostat, microfilm, xerography, or any other means, or
incorporated into any information retrieval system,
electronic or mechanical, without the written permission
of the copyright owner.

All inquiries should be addressed to
Barron's Educational Series, Inc.
250 Wireless Boulevard
Hauppauge, NY 11788

International Standard Book No. 0-8120-3793-6

Library of Congress Catalog Card No.

Library of Congress Cataloging-in-Publication Data

PRINTED IN THE UNITED STATES OF AMERICA

8   9770   98765432

Contents

Preface 5

Should You Buy a Golden Retriever? 6
Making an Intelligent Choice 6
An Adult or a Puppy? 7
Selecting the Right Puppy for You 8
Where and How to Buy a Golden Retriever 8
How Much Will It Cost? 9

Housing and Supplies 10
Indoor Space Requirements 10
Keeping Your Golden Outdoors 11
Additional Equipment and Accessories 12
Dog Toys 14

Caring for a Golden Retriever 15
Before the Puppy Comes Home 15
The First Days Home 15
Grooming a Golden Retriever 16
    Equipment 16
    Coat Care 16
    Bathing 19
    Nail and Tooth/Ear and Eye Care 19
Lifting and Carrying a Golden Retriever 20
Golden Retrievers and Children 21
    The Golden and the New Baby 21
Goldens and Other Pets 22
The Social Behavior of Dogs 22
Social Considerations for a Female Dog 22
Vacationing with Your Golden Retriever 23
    Feeding Your Vacationing Dog 24

Proper Nutrition 25
Understanding Nutrition 25
The Basic Nutrient Groups 25
    Protein 25
    Fat 25
    Carbohydrates 25
    Vitamins 26
    Minerals 26
    Trace Elements 26
    Water 26
Commercial Dog Foods 26
Feeding by Age 27
    Puppies under Five Months Old 27
    Puppies Five to Seven Months Old 27

Puppies Seven to Ten Months Old 27
Feeding Adult Dogs 27

Ailments and Illnesses 29
Understanding Symptoms 29
    Vomiting 29
    Diarrhea 29
Preventive Medicine 29
    Vaccinations 29
    Preventing Infectious Diseases 30
    Vaccination Schedule 31
Of Worms and Worming 31
External Parasites 33
Of Mites and Mange 34
Other Skin Disorders 34
Digestive Disorders 37
    Constipation 37
    Enteritis 37
    Tonsillitis 37
Respiratory Ailments 37
Eye Disorders 37
Ear Ailments 38
Other Disorders 38
    Hip Dysplasia 38
    False Pregnancy 38
    Shock 39
    Poisoning 39
Nursing a Sick Dog 40

Breeding Golden Retrievers 42
Breeding Objectives 42
Characteristics of the Golden Retriever 42
    General Appearance 42
    Deviations from Breed Characteristics 45
Breeding Your Golden Female 46
    Choosing a Mate 46
    When Is the Female Ready? 46
The Birth of Puppies 47
Care of Puppies 47
Dog Shows and Exhibitions 48

Basic and Advanced Training 50
Why Dogs Learn 50
Basic Rules of Training 50
Training a Puppy 51
    Housebreaking 51

Contents

Walking on a Leash 52
Begging Is Forbidden 52
Being Alone 52
Simple Commands 52
Training for the Obedience Ring 56
Using Obedience Schools for Training 56
Heeling 57
Relinquishing an Object 58
Lying Down 58
Retrieving 58
Jumping over Hurdles 58
Problems in Training 59
Field Trials 59
Guide Dog Training 59

Understanding the Golden Retriever 61
Origins and Early History 61
The Golden Retriever in the United States 61
The Nature of the Golden Retriever 62
Behavior Problems 65
What Your Dog Can Tell You 65
The Sense Organs 65
From Puppy to Adult Dog 66
Encounters in the Outside World 66
How Your Dog Affects You 67

Useful Address 68

Index 69

Preface

When Sir Dudley Marjoriebanks, the first Lord Tweedmouth, developed the golden retriever, he could not have foreseen the breed becoming as popular as it is today. To dog authorities, however, the reason for this popularity is obvious.

The golden is one of the greatest of all hunting dogs. It has the scenting power of the bloodhound, as well as all of the abilities of a setter and a retriever. This breed is extremely successful on land, but its greatest ability is in retrieving from water. The golden has a soft mouth, and it is able to withstand the temperatures of the coldest ponds and streams. It is hardy, proud, tough, and shows great endurance—all of which makes it an ideal companion for the sportsman.

Like most hunting dogs, goldens are easy to train. They are eager learners, extremely obedient, and very patient. These factors have made the golden retriever very popular among sportsmen and a dominant breed in both the field and the obedience ring.

Although originally bred for hunting, the golden, through generations of careful breeding and the influence of the close human-canine relationship, has developed a unique temperament. Few breeds can match the golden's friendly, loving, and gentle nature; fewer still display its innate love for children. In addition, goldens are naturally clean, easy to groom, and suffer from few genetic diseases. All of these qualities make the golden retriever an ideal family pet.

The physical characteristics and temperament of the golden retriever make it a truly unique breed.

Unfortunately, in recent years it has been shown that these traits cannot be taken for granted. The increase in the golden's popularity has led to careless breeding practices by people whose primary concern is for profits. As a result of these practices, an increasing number of goldens suffer from physical and behavioral problems.

This practical manual will tell you everything you need to know about choosing and raising a golden retriever. It will answer your questions about keeping a dog in your house or in a kennel. Detailed instructions tell you how to help the dog adapt to its new home and how to feed and care for it. This manual also provides information about preventive medicine, symptoms of illness, and treatment of various injuries and diseases.

A chapter traces the breed's origin and history, describes the basic behavioral patterns of goldens, as well as of dogs in general, and outlines the breed standard. There is also a chapter devoted entirely to training your golden retriever. For novice dog owners, it provides the fundamentals of instruction needed to develop a sound program for daily practice sessions. It is also hoped that experienced owners may find new ideas to incorporate into their daily regimen.

I would like to acknowledge the assistance of Matthew Vriends, PhD, consulting editor of this series, and Helgard Niewisch, DVM, who read the manuscript and made invaluable suggestions.

Jaime J. Sucher

Should You Buy a Golden Retriever?

Making an Intelligent Choice

Golden retrievers have quickly become one of the most popular pure breed dogs in America. Although originally bred for hunting, goldens have shown tremendous versatility, and they excel in other areas as well. They have been used by authorities in searching out explosives and narcotics, and have proven to be reliable Seeing-Eye dogs. However, in recent years, goldens have made their greatest impact as family pets.

The popularity of the golden retriever, to an extent, is very much a reflection of our modern society's concept of the perfect family dog. It is a very attractive breed that requires a minimum of grooming to keep it in "show" condition. Goldens are reasonably clean, and they are very easy to maintain in top physical and mental health. They also possess the ideal temperament for a family dog.

Goldens are "people" dogs. They are a friendly, gentle, and eager breed that truly need human companionship. Anyone who takes the time and

Golden retrievers combine the abilities of a great hunting dog with the gentle, loving nature of an ideal household pet.

effort to establish a positive rapport with a golden will be rewarded with a loving and affectionate friend that will do anything to please his or her master.

Goldens are easy to train because they really love to learn. Their favorite time may well be the training session. This breed has the ability to learn practically anything a human can teach a dog to do. This trait has made them a popular hunting dog as well as a dominant force in the obedience ring.

Although these qualities may be found in all goldens, the owner must be sure they are developed and become part of the dog's personality. Bringing out the best in your dog will take time, energy, patience, and understanding.

To buy, or not to buy, a golden retriever is an important decision. Many people who purchase dogs are not aware of all the responsibilities of dog ownership at the time of purchase. This lack of awareness usually results in an unhappy relationship for both dog and owner. Therefore, before you buy a golden retriever, carefully consider the following points:

- First and foremost, are you looking for a watchdog? If the answer is "yes," then the golden retriever is not for you. As stated earlier, the golden retriever is renowned for its gentleness, an undesirable trait in a watchdog. A golden retriever may bark at a stranger at the door, but its tail will be wagging as an invitation to play.
- Do you have the time, energy, and patience required to raise a dog properly? If you purchase a golden puppy, would you be willing and able to adjust your schedule to meet the dog's needs?
- Are you willing to devote some of your free time to the dog? Do you travel on weekends or take long vacations? Are you willing to travel only to areas where you can bring your golden retriever? Remember that although dogs can withstand the stress of travel fairly well, they are prohibited in many hotels and motels.
- Do you understand the long-term commitment involved in owning a golden retriever? A dog should never be purchased impulsively, especially because a golden may live a dozen years or more

• Do you have a large yard, or is there a park or woods nearby where your dog can get its much-needed exercise? A golden is a remarkable breed and can adapt to any living quarters that can sensibly house a medium-large breed. However, because the golden is bred for hunting, exercise is an important part of its physical and mental well-being.

• Finally, can you afford to keep a golden retriever? Aside from the initial expenses of buying the dog and purchasing necessary supplies, the cost of feeding may go as high as $40 per month. And don't forget additional expenses such as annual visits to the veterinarian.

You should consider these questions carefully before you buy a golden retriever. Find out if there is a chapter of the Golden Retriever Club of America in your area. This organization can help answer any questions you may have. Remember, owning a dog of any breed is a serious responsibility. If you do not care for the dog properly, its health and happiness will suffer, and you will not experience the pleasure and satisfaction of raising a golden retriever.

An Adult or a Puppy?

One of the great rewards of owning a golden retriever is watching it grow from an awkward, tiny bundle of fur into a thoroughly trained, well-behaved, beautiful adult. However, this requires a great deal of patience, time, and energy. If you work diligently with your puppy during the early training phases, you will be rewarded with the most loving four-legged companion imaginable. However, if your puppy is given little training, it may grow up to be eighty pounds of unruly hyper-activity—a situation that no dog owner could cope with for very long.

Therefore, selecting an adult golden also offers advantages. A well-trained adult makes a marvelous pet. It can save you the time and effort needed for rearing and training a puppy. Mature goldens almost always adapt easily to new owners and environments. A housebroken, trained adult golden makes an ideal companion for owners for whom raising puppies may be too much work. The greatest drawback to buying an older golden is that you may find it extremely difficult to correct any bad habits the dog has already acquired.

When choosing between a golden puppy and an adult, keep in mind that raising a puppy will allow you to train it to the habits of your home. Adult dogs, on the other hand, need significantly less attention, which means less work and effort, especially for an older owner.

If you are looking for a show dog, you have two options. First, you can purchase a potential show puppy from a reputable breeder and raise it yourself. This way you will have the satisfaction of knowing that you have done the job yourself. If you do not need this satisfaction, you can purchase a mature show dog; this way you are assured of your golden's quality and beauty.

Whether you choose a puppy or an adult is an extremely important decision. However, the choice of the sex of the dog is not always as important. Golden females (bitches) are just as good a choice as males. Females are usually only slightly smaller and lighter than males. In addition, there is no significant difference in temperament between the sexes.

The only time you might prefer a specific sex is if you are interested in breeding the dog. If you are considering starting a kennel, females are preferable. If you select a female and have no intention of breeding her, have the dog spayed. Because there are an alarming number of homeless dogs in the United States, owners should take all possible precautions against the needless proliferation of unwanted animals. Another advantage of spaying is avoiding the messiness that will occur when she is "in heat." The female will also be more likely to avoid breast tumors, ovarian cysts, false pregnancies, and other ailments if she has been spayed.

Note that if you plan to enter your female in a dog show, she will be disqualified if she is spayed. A spayed dog, however, may compete in field and obedience trials.

Should You Buy a Golden Retriever

Selecting the Right Puppy for You

While visiting all the reputable breeders on your list, pay special attention to the following factors. Above all, a golden must be healthy and possess a temperament typical of the breed. When you first look at a puppy, you will see only an adorable, energetic bundle of fur and wrinkles. Learn to see past this, and resist the impulse to buy the first puppy that catches your fancy. Examine the puppy's coat; it should be smooth and shiny. Its eyes should be bright and have a friendly and curious expression. It should be solidly built. Remember also that goldens are very people-oriented, and this should be obvious even at an early age. Look for an eager, alert puppy with a wagging tail, and avoid both hyperactive and overly sedate dogs.

Another good indicator of the puppy's temperament is its mother's behavior. After all, many of the puppy's behavioral characteristics are inherited from its sire (father) or dam (mother). Observe how the mother reacts to people. She should be friendly and show no signs of fear or apprehension.

If the puppy appears to be in good health and of sound temperament, the next step is to check its pedigree papers. These papers are a written record of the dog's recent ancestry. Like most medium and large breeds, some bloodlines of goldens suffer from hip dysplasia. Many breeders will have their dogs examined for this disease by the Orthopedic Foundation of Animals (OFA). Dogs that are free of this ailment are given an OFA number that is placed on the pedigree. In addition, numbers are given to dogs that have had their eyes checked and cleared. Never purchase a dog whose pedigree papers lack these numbers.

If the dog's pedigree is satisfactory, ask the breeder for the date the puppy was wormed, and be sure to get a written record of this for later use by your veterinarian. Do not be afraid to ask questions of the breeder. A reputable breeder is just as concerned with the puppy's welfare as you are. Also, do not be offended if the breeder asks questions about your experience with dogs and where you plan to raise your puppy. Take this as a sign of concern. In addition, keep an open line of communication with the breeder so that he or she can help you with any future problems.

When you have finally chosen a breeder, you must then choose your puppy. As previously mentioned, at first all puppies will look cute and very much alike. Watch them carefully, however, and their subtle differences will become more apparent. By watching them play together, you can get a better idea of their individual temperaments. Some may be bolder, others shyer; the puppy's temperament is the best indicator of its adult behavior. Again, do not hesitate to ask the breeder for help.

Where and How to Buy a Golden Retriever

The first thing to do when searching for a good-quality golden retriever is to visit each of the well-established golden kennels in your area. The secretary of the Golden Retriever Club of America, your local Golden Club, or the American Kennel Club can all help you obtain a list of registered and reputable breeders in your area. Make appointments at each of these kennels in order to inspect the dogs, the conditions in which they are kept, and their basic breeding stock. It is best to visit as many kennels as possible, regardless of their distance, since it is important to get a healthy, well-cared-for dog. The time you spend finding the right dog will save you a great deal of effort and heartbreak later on.

Remember that the quality of your puppy will be a direct reflection of the quality of the breeder. Conscientious breeders will make every effort to satisfy you in order to maintain their reputation.

You should never be tempted to buy a "cheap" dog. The old adage, "You get what you pay for," is all too true in purchasing a dog. A lower-priced dog may mean it was raised strictly for profit by an inexperienced breeder, or that it is in poor health. You should also avoid kennels that are not dedicated solely to raising golden retrievers. Breeders who raise several breeds are not always knowledgeable about the special needs of each breed.

Once you have selected the puppy that is best for you, you will have to arrange to take it home. The puppy should be seven weeks old when it moves into its new home. A puppy of this age should adapt very easily to its new environment, yet it should not be old enough to have picked up many bad habits. Recent studies have shown that during their eighth week, puppies become especially sensitive to environmental changes. If you cannot pick up the puppy during the seventh week, wait until the ninth week. Rather than risk behavioral problems, wait until the puppy is ready for change.

If you live within a reasonable distance of the breeder, pick up the puppy yourself. However, if the distance makes this impossible, the dog will have to be shipped. Many people feel that the shipping of dogs is a cruel and irresponsible act that can cause psychological damage. In recent years, however, dog shipping has become common, and it can be done with few or no problems. Although I encourage you to pick up your puppy yourself, if you are faced with the choice of shipping a dog or buying one from a questionable breeder, by all means ship the dog.

How Much Will It Cost?

The initial purchase price of a golden retriever varies; however, expect to spend at least $200. Puppies from champion caliber parents may sell for as much as $1000 or more. A younger puppy will usually be less expensive than an older dog, because the breeder will have invested less time and money in it. The closer an older puppy is to being a show dog, the more expensive it will be. Remember that the extra money you spend initially may save you a great deal of money on veterinary bills, as well as the heartache that accompanies a poorly reared dog. Licensing fees

also vary greatly, so check with your local town hall or animal shelter.

As stated earlier, food may cost as much as $40 a month, and you must also purchase certain equipment for feeding, grooming, and housing your dog. Veterinarian costs must also be considered. A dog requires annual immunizations against all infectious diseases, as well as an annual heartworm test. A puppy may also have to be wormed. If your dog should get sick or injured, it may need additional, costly medical attention.

Finally, you will have to pay a fee to register your dog with the American Kennel Club, as well as annual dues if you join the Golden Retriever Club of America.

You can see that the expenses of owning a golden retriever are much greater than the initial purchase price. Therefore, carefully consider these costs before you buy a dog.

Indoor Space Requirements

A golden retriever, whether a puppy or an adult, needs a reasonably spacious, quiet living area where it can feel comfortable and secure. Inside your home you must provide the dog with a "territory" of its own. This territory will represent your dog's feeding and sleeping areas. In order for your dog to feel protected, these areas should not be moved. A dog will only feel secure if it has a quiet, reliable place to rest undisturbed. This area should neither isolate the dog nor should it be subject to heavy human traffic.

Good resting areas are most often found in corners where the dog is protected on two sides. These areas should also be draft-free and not in direct sunlight. The dog's sleeping area should also make it easy to confine its movements when you go to bed or when you leave the house.

Your choice of a sleeping box and pad, or a cage with pad, will depend on your method of housebreaking. (See the chapter entitled, "Basic and Advanced Training"). I recommend using a cage, as it can also be invaluable for transporting and disciplining your puppy. Dogs are instinc-

Whelping box and sleeping baskets. Make certain that the one you make or choose is large enough for a full-grown golden to lie down in comfortably.

tively den animals, and the confined space of a cage will make a puppy feel safer and more comfortable than an open sleeping box.

The cage should be approximately 24 inches (61 cm) high, by 24 inches (61 cm) wide, by 36 inches (91 cm) long. The construction of the cage is important, for it must have strong welds that cannot be broken by a large, active puppy.

The cage will be your puppy's "house" when you are not around to supervise it. Some cases can also be used to carry your puppy when you go for a drive or to the veterinarian.

If you decide not to use a cage, purchase a sleeping box. Make sure it is large enough to accommodate a full-grown, spread-out dog. Line the box with cedar shavings and shredded newspapers and then place an old blanket over it. Your dog will find this very comfortable for sleeping. If you decide to build your own box, use only non-splintering hardwoods. Because many stains and paints are toxic to puppies, leave the box unfinished.

Several types of dog carriers are available. Small carriers with a single handle (top left) are suitable for golden puppies. An adult golden would require a larger carrier, such as the wire cage on a platform (lower right).

10

Like its sleeping place, a dog's feeding place should never be changed. Changes in sleeping and feeding places can cause your pet unnecessary stress. An animal under stress may exhibit behavioral changes as well as changes in many biological functions, including problems with digestion and excretion. Place your dog's feeding areas in an easily cleaned room such as the kitchen.

Keeping Your Golden Outdoors

When you are not home, your golden will be just as happy (if not happier) outdoors as inside your home. Because a golden retriever is family-oriented, do not keep your dog outdoors for very long periods when you are home. If you are outside working, by all means, bring your dog with you. During these outdoor periods your golden will get its daily exercise.

If you leave your dog outside when you are not home, provide it with a fenced enclosure or run. The run should be at least 6 feet (2 m) wide, by 15 feet (5 m) long, by 6 feet (2 m) high, and it should be constructed of strong chain link fence. You can place partially buried boards around the bottom to

The doghouse. Hinging the roof panels facilitates cleaning and airing.

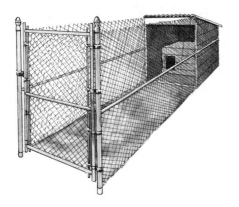

This type of run, complete with shelter, provides your dog with a place to exercise as well as protection from rain, snow, wind, and direct sunlight.

prevent the dog from digging under the fence. The run can be as large as your yard. However, it must not be smaller than the size stated.

Use a few inches of smooth stone as a base. This will provide drainage when it rains, and it will prevent the dog from becoming muddy. Do not use concrete as a floor because concrete will retain the smell of urine. The run must also provide your dog with some shade and shelter.

The best form of outdoor shelter is a doghouse. Whether you build your own or buy one, make sure it is raised several inches off the ground to avoid dampness and insects. The doghouse must be properly constructed to protect the dog against wind, rain, and cold, for even a minor draft can lead to serious respiratory ailments. The doghouse should be approximately 48 inches (122 cm) long, 36 inches (91 cm) high, and 36 inches (91 cm) wide. If the house is too small, the dog will not be able to stand or sleep comfortably. Also, be sure not to make the house overly large because during cold weather the dog's body will provide the only form of heat. For this reason, it is also best to insulate the structure.

You can take several precautions in order to keep the house clean. Place a hinged roof on the house for better access. Line the floor with an easy-to-clean material, such as linoleum, above the flooring so that you can spread cedar shavings and cover them with a blanket.

Finally, make sure that the opening of the house faces south and is not subject to the cold north winds of winter. You can also hang a piece of canvas or blanket over the opening, making sure it overlaps sufficiently to eliminate drafts. If you live in a climate where winter nights can be very cold, I recommend that you find an indoor place where the dog can sleep—unless you have carefully tested the insulation of the doghouse.

Additional Equipment and Accessories

Your puppy's first day at home can be very busy and hectic. To avoid additional work and confusion, purchase the following items and keep them available.

The most important pieces of equipment, at least from your dog's point of view, are its food

Several types of food and water dishes are available. All are sturdy; some include food and water dishes in the same stand.

Collars come in all shapes and sizes and can be made of chain (above), leather, or nylon (below). Collars with slip rings (above) are excellent for training a golden.

and water dishes. They should be nonbreakable and heavy, as well as sturdy enough so that a golden with a voracious appetite cannot tip them over. Bowls are available in plastic, stainless steel, and ceramic. If you choose a ceramic bowl, make sure it was not fired with a lead-based glaze.

You may have to purchase more than one collar for your dog as it matures. A puppy needs a light collar but not necessarily a strong one. A small puppy requires only a leather or nylon collar, but bear in mind that these tend to deteriorate with time. In addition, your puppy's neck size will increase considerably as it grows, and not all collars adjust sufficiently. Chain collars are strong enough for an adult golden. I recommend buying your puppy an inexpensive leather or nylon collar and changing to a good chain collar when the dog is nearly full grown. I also recommend purchasing reflecting tags or tape for your dog's collar and leash. These make it easier for a driver to see both dog and master when headlights shine on them, thus making nighttime walks much safer. You should also attach an identity tag with your address and phone number to the dog's collar. This could prove invaluable if your dog ever becomes lost.

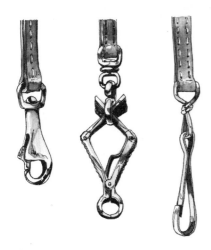

The long or reel leash enables you to adjust the free play when walking your golden.

Leaves can attach to collars using a safety catch (left), scissor clip (center), or regular spring clip (right).

Leashes come in a wide variety of lengths and materials, and you may want to purchase more than one type. For regular walks, use a leash only a few feet long. This will enable you to quickly bring the dog to your side if you need to. It will also keep the dog from straying too far. If you have sufficient yard space, a 30-foot (10 m) leash with an automatic reel is useful. Remember that golden puppies will chew—or attempt to chew—anything near their mouths. Therefore, you should not purchase a chain leash for a puppy. Chewing on the chain may damage your puppy's teeth.

Flea spray and tweezers are helpful in case of external parasites. Flea sprays include aerosols, pump-on liquids, and alcohol-based liquids that you can rub on. Flea powders and collars are also available. You will need tweezers to remove ticks.

Golden retriever owners seldom need muzzles for their dogs. However, you should keep one easily accessible, should the need arise. Some foreign countries require all dogs to wear muzzles, so if you are planning such a trip with your golden, you may need one. A muzzle is also a good precaution if your dog is hurt and you must bring it to a veterinarian. A dog in severe pain may react unpredictably, so be prepared. When buying a muzzle, be sure you get one that can be adjusted for size. Remember that there is a big difference between the head of a golden puppy and that of an adult.

A muzzle may be legally required in areas where there is a rabies outbreak.

Dog Toys

Toys are essential to a dog's well-being. They signify play to a dog, and they let it know that life comprises more than training sessions, eating, and sleeping. Playing with toys gives a dog exercise. In addition, they allow a puppy to develop its survival instincts, as it will attempt to stalk and capture its toys. Giving your puppy toys will also spare your furniture and clothing from teethmarks.

Rawhide bones are excellent for strengthening a golden's teeth and jaw muscles. A puppy's teeth can quickly chew through rawhide. Therefore, make sure to replace the bone before it becomes small enough for your puppy to swallow it whole. Avoid toys your puppy can shred and swallow, for they can cause choking or a blockage in the stomach.

When choosing toys, make sure they are designed for dogs and are made of non-toxic materials. Some forms of plastic are toxic, and many forms of wood splinter. In addition, be careful with painted items. Some older types of paint contain lead, which if swallowed in excess can be poisonous and even fatal. To be safe, avoid all painted or varnished toys.

A golden puppy will chew almost anything that will fit into its mouth. It will also tend to seek out anything with your scent, such as your old shoes and clothing. For this reason, keep these items out of your puppy's reach. Also, never give your puppy either your old slippers or toys that resemble valuable objects. To a golden puppy, there is little difference between a toy slipper and a real one. This is true of anything of value to you: letters, money, keys, baseball gloves, and so on. Keep all valuable items away from your puppy, and you will prevent the development of bad habits.

If you are looking for toys around your house, I recommend cardboard boxes, shopping bags, and large balls such as tennis balls. (Golf balls, ping pong balls, and the like should not be used because they can be chewed apart and swallowed). These simple household objects can entertain a puppy for hours.

Caring for a Golden Retriever

Before the Puppy Comes Home

Take a few steps now to reduce the confusion when you bring your puppy home. In addition to purchasing necessary equipment and accessories, you should also choose the puppy's food and purchase a supply of it.

When you have bought all the supplies and have placed them in readily accessible locations, begin to "puppy-proof" your home. Remember that a young puppy is very curious, and as it roams through your house it will sniff, paw at, and chew almost everything. For this reason, place all potential hazards out of the puppy's reach.

Remove all poisons, including paints, cleaners, disinfectants, insecticides, and antifreeze. Store them in an area your puppy will have absolutely no access to. Also, remove all sharp objects such as broken glass, nails, and staples. If you have an older home, make sure your dog does not eat paint chips containing lead.

Electrical wires must also be moved out of your puppy's reach. A dog chewing on electrical wires can be injured or killed by the resulting shock.

The First Days Home

Have you ever had to adjust to a new environment such as a different house, a college dorm, or an apartment? You probably remember feeling loneliness from missing loved ones and friends, and confusion or bewilderment about your new surroundings. In addition, you may have been excited about your new home and your upcoming adventures there. In the same way, the first days home are a very emotional time for your puppy, for it has just entered an unfamiliar world, apart from its mother and siblings.

The first hours in your home are very important ones for your puppy. At seven weeks of age a golden puppy is very impressionable. If a frenzied horde of family and friends greet it at the door, the puppy will believe that hysterical behavior is readily accepted in your home. Introduce your puppy to its new home carefully so it will believe it is entering a safe, calm, rational environment.

When your puppy arrives, it will probably want to urinate or defecate. Instead of entering your house, walk the puppy to a place you have chosen for its elimination area. Give the puppy about ten minutes to relieve itself, and then praise and pet it for doing so. This will help the puppy learn to defecate and urinate outdoors.

In order to help the puppy adjust, let it sniff around your home undisturbed. Then help it learn the location of its food and water dishes. Let your puppy continue to roam about, but feel free to pet it and play with it. When it tires, pick it up and put it in its sleeping box or cage. Within a few days, the puppy should learn where its sleeping area is, and when tired, find its bed on its own.

To me, the next step in training your puppy is the hardest test you will face. Furthermore, it is your first test, and failure here will mean greater problems in the future. Your puppy will probably whine, whimper, and wail, because it is in an unfamiliar place and because it misses its mother and siblings. It is important, however, that you remain firm. If the puppy sleeps in a cage, do not let it out. If you do, it will wail every time it wants to leave the cage. If you use a sleeping box, you might try to reassure the puppy by speaking softly, but do not take it from the box. Your puppy must learn to deal with loneliness as soon as possible.

When feeding your puppy, you should follow a few fundamental rules. First, be sure to feed your puppy the same kind of food used by the breeder. Changes in surroundings will cause the puppy a certain amount of stress, which may affect its digestive system. By not changing its diet, you will avoid digestive problems. Second, try to feed your puppy on the same schedule used by the breeder. However, if that schedule is inconvenient, change the feeding times slowly to meet your schedule. Finally, never bother your dog while it is eating (or sleeping). A dog that is surprised may sometimes act unpredictably. Be sure to also explain this rule to your children.

Caring for A Golden Retriever

If you must leave the house during your puppy's first few days, be sure it is not left alone. If no family member is available, ask a neighbor or a close friend to "puppy-sit." An unsupervised, curious golden retriever puppy means only one thing: a mess. Your puppy will investigate its surroundings, using all its instinctive hunting skills. Its keen sense of smell will track down various forms of trouble (perhaps the legs of your coffee table or your dining room curtains). Once it spots a target, the puppy will attempt to render it helpless. It will use teeth, paws, and if necessary, all its body weight to accomplish this feat. Hopefully, you will return before the puppy decides to mark off its territory.

Soon after your puppy arrives, you must begin to train it. Training will require time, energy, patience, understanding, and of course, love. From the minute your golden arrives, begin to teach it its name. Other essential lessons are described in detail in the chapter, "Basic and Advanced Training." Remember, the longer you wait to begin training, the harder it will be for your dog to learn.

Grooming a Golden Retriever

Grooming your golden retriever is a simple task that should take no more than about a half hour. You should groom the dog at least once every two weeks.

Equipment
You will need the following equipment to keep your dog in top condition: a pin brush, slicker brush, comb, shears, nail clippers, and styptic powder.

Coat Care
Start by giving your dog a thorough brushing. Use a slicker brush for the major portions of its body. Use a pin brush for the feathering on the legs, chest, and tail. After brushing, comb the entire coat to remove any loose hairs. By brushing first,

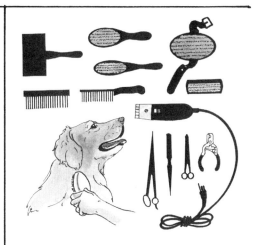

Daily grooming is important for your golden. After a thorough combing to remove tangles, the dog should be brushed just as thoroughly.

you will remove stubborn tangles and make combing easier.

While brushing, look for signs of external parasites such as fleas and ticks. If you see any, spray or powder the dog immediately. These parasites may be harder to eliminate if you leave them to multiply. If you note any unusual skin conditions, contact your veterinarian for advice.

Some goldens grow a great deal of soft hair on or around their ears, which may be trimmed to improve their appearance. In addition, you can trim any long or straggly hair growing around the edge of the ears. You should also trim the hair between the pads of your dog's feet. Cut this hair

Goldens are people dogs. Whether fetching a stick or spending a lazy morning with a child, the golden is at its best when it has human companionship.

as short as possible. This will reduce the chance of infection in damp weather, and will also improve the dog's traction. Trim the dog's feathering if it becomes excessively long.

Bathing

The golden retriever is a double-coated breed. Excessive bathing will promote shedding of the undercoat, so bathe your dog only when necessary. If the dog's underside or legs are dirty, wash them with a wet, soapy cloth.

When a bath is necessary, purchase a high-quality dog shampoo. After shampooing, be sure to rinse out the shampoo thoroughly. Soap that is not rinsed out may irritate your dog's skin. If you wish, use a cream rinse to give the coat more body and make the hair easier to comb. Then towel the dog dry. Rub the dog briskly with a large towel in order to remove most of the water. Then brush and comb its coat. Keep the dog indoors and away from drafts while it is drying.

Nail and Tooth/Ear and Eye Care

If your dog is active and gets plenty of exercise, you will not need to trim its nails regularly. However, nails can grow back quickly on a "house dog," which may require frequent trimming. Before you trim your dog's nails, be sure you learn how to use a pair of clippers. Improper use of nail clippers can cause your dog a great deal of pain. An experienced dog groomer or a veterinarian can show you how to use them. The center of a dog's nail (called the "quick") contains a blood vessel and nerve endings. You can see these when you examine the dog's claws. If you cut the quick, your dog will suffer much pain.

The quick grows out as your dog's nail lengthens. If you wait too long between pedicures, you

These well-behaved dogs await patiently for their turn to perform at obedience school. These schools, which are conducted in an atmosphere that is optimal for learning, can help you and your golden establish a good training routine.

Clipping nails. Several types of clippers are available. The guillotine-type, shown here, works well.

may have to cut the quick in order to clip the nail back to a comfortable length. Always clip the nail as close to the quick as possible. If you accidentally cut the nail too short, it will bleed. Stop the bleeding by using styptic powder.

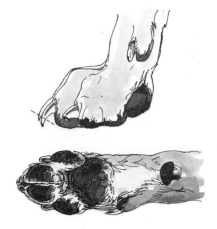

Clip your golden's nails at an angle, making sure not to cut the "quick."

Proper tooth care means feeding your dog plenty of hard foods such as dog biscuits and suitable meat bones or rawhide bones. These foods help prevent the buildup of tartar which, if left untreated, can cause deterioration of the gums and loss of teeth. In addition, a little lemon juice or fresh tomatoes in your dog's food will help prevent the formation of tartar. Clean your dog's teeth weekly by brushing them with a toothbrush soaked in lemon juice. Thick tartar buildup can be scraped off by your veterinarian.

Ear and eye care are very important; however, I recommend that you first consult a veterinarian for the proper way to clean and care for them. An inexperienced owner can harm a dog seriously by probing around its ears and eyes. The veterinarian can show you how to clean dirt and wax out of the ear and how to clean any sticky discharge that often collects in the corner of a dog's eye. Once you have learned these procedures, you will be able to care for these sensitive organs with confidence.

When checking your golden's eyes, do not put your hands or fingers too close to the sensitive eyeballs. By gently pulling on the skin above and below the eye, you can expose enough of the area to observe the eye without harming your dog.

Lifting and Carrying a Golden Retriever

It is very important for everyone in your family to learn how to lift and carry your puppy. Improper

The proper way to lift and carry your puppy. Support the puppy's rear and hind legs with one hand, and hold its chest with the other.

handling can hurt and possibly injure the dog. Place one hand under the puppy's chest and support the rear and hind legs with the other hand. Never pick up the puppy by placing only one hand under its abdomen, and never pick it up by the scruff of the neck. Both of these methods can hurt the puppy.

You should carry an adult golden only if it is injured or sick. When moving an injured dog, take special precautions. If possible, wait for an experienced person to lift and carry the dog. If you must do this yourself, first place a muzzle on the dog, for a dog in pain may act unpredictably and snap at anyone who tries to help it. Place both of your arms between the dog's four legs and lift. Do not allow the dog's midsection to sag or its head to fall forward. If the dog's weight and size are too great for you, lay it on its side on a blanket or stretcher, and carry it with the help of another person. For further information on treating an injured dog, consult the chapter, "If Your Dog Gets Sick."

Golden Retrievers and Children

One of the greatest pleasures of owning a golden retriever is watching it play with children. A mature golden seems to know instinctively that children are more fragile than adults, and it will be more gentle when playing with youngsters. Younger and more excitable goldens may have trouble controlling their natural exuberance when playing with children. A golden puppy plays rambunctiously both with its littermates and with children. Therefore, when a young dog plays with children, it should always be supervised.

A special bond forms between a golden and children. Golden retrievers tolerate tremendous pushing, pulling, pinching, and ear and tail tugging from boisterous children. In fact, they seem to enjoy the attention more than they mind the pain. The golden's coat and skin are extremely tough, for a hunting dog must be able to cope with all types of weather and to run through dense woods and thickets.

However, because the golden does have vulnerable areas such as its eyes and nose, teach your children the proper way to handle their pet. Children should be taught to never disturb a golden while it is eating or sleeping. Explain that although the dog is a loving pet, it may nip at them if surprised or frightened. Also teach your children how to meet a strange dog. They should

A boy and his golden enjoy one last loving moment together before bedtime.

not go to the dog, but let it approach them. They should not move suddenly, and they should keep their hands below the dog's head. If the dog sniffs their hands, and is still friendly, it is all right to pet it.

You can help assure an enduring relationship between your children and your golden by involving them in the responsibilities of dog care. Encourage your children to help feed, groom, and walk your dog.

The Golden and the New Baby

Reports of attacks on infants by family dogs lead many people to get rid of their devoted pets when they have a new baby. This is truly a shame, for goldens are at their best when they have children —including infants—to love. If you have or are planning to have a baby, take heart. Animal behavior experts who have studied this problem thoroughly have concluded that most dogs will not be aggressive toward a baby. They also believe, however, that dogs that tend to chase and kill small animals, or those that are aggressive toward people in general, should never be left unsupervised with an infant.

You should take several precautions to make sure your golden will readily accept your new baby. Train your dog to sit or lie down for long periods of time before the baby is born. As you increase the length of time the dog remains still, accustom it to other activities occurring around it at the same time. Reward your dog if it stays still and does not attempt to follow you.

Once training is complete, simulate the other activities that will occur after the baby arrives. Use a doll to imitate carrying, feeding, changing, and bathing the newborn.

After the birth of the infant, give the dog something the baby used in the hospital in order for it to sniff, smell, and become accustomed to the baby's scent. Upon returning home from the hospital, allow the mother to greet the dog without the baby. Then place the baby in the nursery and deny the dog access by using a screen door or folding gate. In this way the dog can see and hear the infant and get used to its presence before they actually meet.

When you finally introduce dog and baby, one person should control and reward the dog while another person holds the baby. Have the dog sit and then show it to the baby. Keep them together for as long as the dog remains calm. For the next week or two, gradually increase the length of the dog's visit.

Never allow your dog to wander unsupervised in the presence of an infant. However, be sure to include your dog in all the activities that involve your newborn. Do not let the dog feel neglected because of the infant. The more activities in which you allow the dog to participate, the stronger the bond will be between golden and child.

Goldens and Other Pets

Goldens get along very well with all other pets. Your golden will rarely show signs of jealousy as long as it receives sufficient attention. If there is a substantial size difference, such as with birds, hamsters, gerbils, and so on, it is best not to allow these animals to play freely with your golden.

If you own two goldens, you will rarely have any problems; in fact, the dogs will probably enjoy each other's companionship. You must remember, however, not to give the older dog any less attention than previously. If you show the older dog that you care for it as much as always, you may leave the two to establish their own relationship. You should have very little difficulty getting the two dogs to live together in harmony. In fact, if you show no favoritism to either dog, the older one should adopt and protect the younger one.

Before buying a second dog, however, remember that you will need additional equipment, including separate sleeping boxes or cages and food dishes. Also be sure you have the extra time, space, and money that a second dog requires.

The Social Behavior of Dogs

If you plan to own more than one golden, or if you wish to understand why dogs react as they do to humans and to each other, you must examine the dog's instinctive nature.

Canine social behavior is very similar to that of wild wolves. Wolves are pack hunting animals and require companionship. This is also true for goldens, though humans can thoroughly satisfy their need for company. Because of this need, you can punish a dog by isolating it during training sessions. In addition, as pack animals, dogs develop among themselves a dominant-subordinate relationship. This relationship allows a stable existence between dogs. Thus, if one of your dogs tends to be more dominant than another, do not worry. This occurs naturally and will prevent fights from breaking out between dogs when competitive situations arise relating to food, living space, and human attention. This social ranking is largely determined by size, age, strength, and sex. This social dominance also allows a dog to obey its master, for during training a dog learns that it is subordinate to the human members of the household.

Both dogs and wolves "mark" their frequently traveled paths or territory by urinating, defecating, and scratching the ground. In addition to such boundary marking, females secrete a scent that signals their being in heat.

Social Considerations for a Female Dog

If you own a female golden, you must take special precautions regarding pregnancy. A golden female normally comes into estrus ("in heat" or "in season") twice a year. Estrus is the period during which the female accepts mating with the male. This period usually lasts 4 to 14 days. If you choose to breed your female, refer to the chapter on breeding and the next section. If you choose not to breed your female, you can take several measures to prevent pregnancy. As stated earlier, if you plan never to breed the female, have her spayed.

The most obvious way to prevent pregnancy, but probably the hardest, is simply to keep your female away from all male dogs. This can be difficult, however, because male dogs will travel a great distance to find a female in heat. During this time, never let your female outside alone, not even in a fenced-in yard. In addition, during this time always walk your female on a leash. The mating urge between the sexes is very great at this time, and the female may be less obedient and not heed your pleas for her to come back.

Many owners who wish to show their females when they are in heat have their veterinarians administer an estrus control medication. This drug, however, may have side effects. Your veterinarian may also administer chlorophyll tablets to help neutralize the odor of the female's secretions.

When a female is in heat, a bloody discharge may spot your floors and rugs. If your children ask about the bleeding, assure them that it is entirely natural. To prevent staining of your rugs or furniture, you may want to confine your female to an easy-to-clean room. Sanitary napkins and diapers are available for dogs in heat. Although you may feel slightly ridiculous or embarrassed about buying them and putting them on your dog, they do help.

Vacationing with Your Golden Retriever

What should you do if you are suddenly called away from home, or if you have planned a vacation and have no family, friends, or neighbors to care for your dog? If you choose not to bring your dog, contact the breeder from whom you purchased it. He or she may be willing to care for it while you are away. If this is not possible, you may wish to place the dog in a boarding kennel. If you plan to do this, be sure to carefully inspect the kennel before leaving your dog there. As previously mentioned, golden retrievers are people-oriented, and many kennels cannot provide the social contact they need. If the kennel can provide the human contact and if the facilities are clean and well managed, a mature golden should have little problem adjusting. You should never leave a puppy younger than six months old at a boarding kennel if you can avoid it.

Of course, you can also take your dog with you. Although this may require some planning and hard work, it can be done. If you plan to travel by air anywhere in the United States or abroad, you'll be glad to know that all major airlines accept dogs. The airline will supply a large crate and will transport your dog in the pressurized cabins of the luggage compartment. Check the cost and any rules concerning pet transport ahead of time.

All major railroads transport dogs throughout the United States. Most will transport large dogs only if they travel in a shipping crate in the baggage car. Check with the railroad to see whether or not they supply the crate.

When traveling by car, your dog may ride either in its cage or in the back seat. Open the window enough to give it some fresh air, but do not expose it to a draft. Drafts can cause eye, ear, and throat problems. Make rest stops at least every two hours and allow your dog to walk and relieve itself. Keep it on a leash so that it will not run away. The inside of a car can get very hot, so allow your dog to drink regularly. Keep a bottle of water on the floor so it remains cool.

Many young dogs become carsick if they are not used to traveling. To prevent this, obtain tablets for motion sickness from your veterinarian.

If you are traveling abroad, obtain a copy of the country's laws pertaining to dogs. Visit or write the consulate of the country you plan to visit, and request a copy. Most countries have minimal requirements concerning dogs; however, some do have special quarantine regulations. You must also be aware of regulations concerning vaccinations, and you will need a valid health certificate from a licensed veterinarian. In addition, you will need a current certificate of vaccination against rabies (not more than six months old). If you need a veterinarian while traveling abroad, you can get a list from the American Consulate or Embassy in the country you are visiting.

Feeding Your Vacationing Dog

When you pack your golden's suitcase for a vacation, remember the following: water dishes, leash, collar, muzzle, blanket (and cage) and brush. If possible, bring enough canned or dry food for the entire trip. If you normally feed your golden fresh meat, accustom it to dry and canned food before you depart. While traveling, your dog may experience additional stress that can affect its digestive system. Therefore, feed your dog only what it is accustomed to, and you should minimize the occurrence of digestive disorders.

Proper Nutrition

Understanding Nutrition

All foods are composed of one or several nutrient groups—proteins, fats, carbohydrates, vitamins, minerals, trace elements, and water. These nutrients are essential for the proper growth and metabolism of a dog. By supplying these nutrients in the correct proportions, you will create a well-balanced diet and insure your dog's proper nutrition.

The type and quantity of nutrients a dog needs depends on several factors. Individual growth rate, the kind of work it does, exercise, metabolism rate, and many environmental factors all influence the quantity of food your dog requires. The amount of food a dog needs changes as it gets older. As a result, a dog may become overweight or underweight if its body requirements have changed but its diet has not. For this reason, you must watch your dog's weight and increase or decrease its food intake when necessary.

The Basic Nutrient Groups

Protein

Protein is one of the most important nutrient groups in your dog's diet. Protein supplies amino acids, which are essential for a healthy dog. Meat, eggs, fish, milk, and cheese are all excellent sources of protein. In addition, you may add other sources of protein such as wheat germ, soybean meals, and brewers dried yeast to your dog's diet. One of the best meat sources of protein is beef, which you may feed your dog either raw or cooked. Cooking does not greatly change the protein value, but it does reduce the fat content somewhat. On the other hand, cooking does break down many vitamins, rendering them of little nutritional value. Be sure you always cook pork before feeding it to your dog. Pigs are primary carriers of Aujeszky's disease, a viral infection that can be fatal to both humans and dogs.

Chicken is a good source of easily digestible protein. Because it takes less energy to digest chicken meat, it is especially good for weak dogs or those recovering from illnesses. When preparing chicken, remove all bones. Chicken bones are soft and tend to splinter when a dog chews them. These splinters can seriously damage a dog's mouth, throat, and digestive tract.

A dog's diet deficient in protein or a specific amino acid may cause poor growth, weight loss, decreased appetite, blood formation problems and edema, and decreased milk production. Protein deficiencies may also result in poor hair and coat condition, and a reduction in antibodies, which can make a dog more susceptible to numerous diseases.

Fat

Fat is a source of energy and heat, and supplies essential fatty acids to a dog's diet. In addition, fat is the primary carrier of fat-soluble vitamins (A, D, and E) and has been shown to make food more palatable for dogs. Fat is also necessary for proper skin and coat development. Fat deficiency usually results in the hair becoming coarse and dry and the appearance of skin lesions. However, the fat found in meat is usually sufficient to meet a dog's needs.

Carbohydrates

Carbohydrates include starches and sugars. They help regulate your golden's energy balance. If a golden's diet lacks carbohydrates, its body will convert proteins normally used for growth into needed sugars. Carbohydrates also supply fibers, which may be digested to supply energy or may help prevent diarrhea by absorbing water in the intestines. Fibers also help prevent constipation and other intestinal problems.

Roughage is another essential carbohydrate. Roughage helps clean a dog's digestive tract so it can more efficiently break down and utilize its food. Some sources of carbohydrates include rice, corn, potatoes, oats, wheat, and cereals. Boiling, toasting, or baking will make it easier for your dog to digest these foods.

Proper Nutrition

Vitamins

Vitamins are extremely important in preventing numerous illnesses and diseases and in regulating many bodily functions such as growth and fertility. Your veterinarian will prescribe the vitamins to add to your dog's diet. An excess of some vitamins may be just as harmful as a deficiency of them. Some good sources of vitamins include brewers yeast, cod liver and wheat germ oils, fresh greens, carrots, and fruits. Many vitamins are unstable and can be destroyed by heat or rancidity. Therefore, serve only fresh, uncooked foods as vitamin supplements.

Minerals

Minerals, like vitamins, aid many body functions. In addition, they help maintain the acid-base balance within a dog's body. The two minerals dogs need most are calcium and phosphorous. These minerals develop strong teeth and bones in puppies and young dogs. You can give your dog sufficient calcium and phosphorous by giving it soft ribs and calf bones to chew on. Calcium phosphate tablets are also available; however, your veterinarian should establish the dosage because too much may be harmful. Salt, another mineral source, is necessary to maintain a proper water balance.

Trace Elements

Trace elements (including cobalt, copper, iodine, iron, manganese, selenium, and zinc) are so named because they are needed only in small quantities. Enough of these elements is found in most foods to meet the needs of a golden retriever.

Water

Water is the most important nutrient because it is vital to all living cells. The body of an adult golden contains nearly 60% water. Because a dog's body cannot store much water, an inadequate supply can quickly cause problems and even death. A dog's water intake depends on such factors as air temperature, type of food, amount of exercise, and temperament. Your dog should have water available at all times, or at least three times a day. Never give your dog a great deal of cold water after a strenuous exercise period, for this can cause water intoxication.

You can purchase commercial dog food that can supply your golden retriever with virtually every essential nutrient. If you wish to prepare your dog's food yourself, however, by all means do so. Just bear in mind that this may be significantly more expensive.

As stated earlier, the quantity of food your dog requires depends on numerous individual and environmental factors. Ask your veterinarian for his or her recommendations regarding a well-balanced, fortified diet.

Commercial Dog Foods

Three types of commercial dog food are available: dry, semi-moist, and canned. Commercial food offers an easy alternative to preparing your dog's meals from scratch. Because dogs are very adaptable, you can choose from many successful commercial formulas, some of which differ greatly in ingredients.

Dry dog foods come in pellets, kibbles, extruded products, or whole biscuits. These foods, as the name suggests, are low in moisture (10 to 12%). They contain mostly grains, cereal by-products, soybean and animal meals, milk products, and fats, as well as vitamin and mineral supplements.

Semi-moist dog foods usually contain between 25 and 30% moisture. These foods generally have added preservatives that protect against spoilage without refrigeration. They contain many of the same ingredients as the dry type, but usually have less meat meals and more whole meat. Semi-moist foods are usually shaped like patties or simulated meat chunks.

Canned dog foods are usually very high in moisture (about 75%). One type is nutritionally complete and can be served alone, while the other is a highly palatable food supplement that you can add to dry foods to make them more appealing.

No matter what type of commercial food you choose, be sure to read the label carefully for nutritional information and feeding tips.

Feeding by Age

Puppies under Five Months Old

Once a puppy is weaned from its mother, it is your responsibility to feed it properly. A puppy requires about twice the nutrients per pound of body weight as an adult dog. Because a puppy grows extremely rapidly, it is important that it get substantial protein. Purchase a high-quality commercial puppy food, and add eggs, diced beef or chicken, milk, or cottage cheese to it. A golden puppy may eat the equivalent of 10% of its body weight daily. Feed a puppy younger than five months old three times a day.

Remember to start feeding your puppy the same food and on the same schedule used by the breeder. Any changes in diet should be made gradually. Always serve your puppy's food at room temperature, and always keep a fresh supply of water in your puppy's dish. Make sure the water is not too cold, especially during the winter, for this can give the puppy chills. Also, be sure to thoroughly wash your puppy's food and water dishes every day. Harmful bacteria can grow quickly in bowls that are not regularly cleaned.

At 14 weeks of age, the puppy's permanent teeth begin to push through the gums, causing pain. To ease the puppy's discomfort, begin to give it a rawhide bone or a large, hard beef bone to chew on. If you don't provide a bone, it may resort to the leg of your coffee table.

Puppies Five to Seven Months Old

At this age, reduce the feedings to two a day. If your dog becomes too fat or too thin, increase or decrease its food intake accordingly. During this period you will probably continue to increase your puppy's food because it is still growing. Add vitamin and mineral supplements in accordance with your veterinarian's advice.

Puppies Seven to Ten Months Old

During this period your dog will begin to reach maturity and will need less food. Continue to give it two meals daily; however, you may begin to serve smaller helpings. Obtain a commercial diet suitable for older puppies and supplement it with meat, chicken, and suitable table scraps.

Feeding Adult Dogs

Coat condition and physical activity are the best indicators of a properly fed dog. A proper diet produces a smooth, soft, shiny coat with rich color. Improperly fed dogs have dull, coarse coats and appear lethargic and fatigued.

How much you feed your adult golden depends on its weight and activity. An outgoing retriever used in hunting needs a higher energy food and more of it than a golden that gets less exercise. In addition, temperament, age, and sex all have a bearing on how much food the dog requires. The best way to monitor how much food your dog needs is to weight it every few weeks. If your dog is gaining weight, reduce its food and fat intake, and give it more exercise.

Environment also has a large bearing on a golden's food intake. A dog kept in an outdoor run in cold weather needs more than 50% more calories than it would if kept in a warm environment.

Although an adult dog is no longer growing, its digestive system needs to be in a steady working condition so the dog may maintain a health metabolism and absorb nutrients properly. To satisfy this need, decrease the protein in your adult dog's diet and increase the carbohydrates. Add carbohydrates high in fiber and roughage in order to clean the intestines and promote healthy digestion.

If you give your dog a well-balanced diet, it will thrive on it for its entire life. A dog will not become tired of the "same old thing" if it is not given a variety of foods. If your dog does not eat, something is wrong emotionally or physically. Although I am not implying that giving your dog a variety of foods is bad, I do wish to point out that loss of appetite indicates a problem. It may be no more than a mild stomach upset; however, if your dog falls off its diet for three or four days, take it to your veterinarian.

Ailments and Illnesses

Understanding Symptoms

Symptoms indicate that your dog is not well and that medical treatment may be necessary. A single symptom, or a combination of them, does not always point to a specific illness. It usually takes the trained eye of a veterinarian to discover the cause of the problem.

Watch for loss of or excessive appetite or thirst, physical exhaustion, poor coat condition, excessive coughing or sneezing, frequent wheezing or running nose, repeated vomiting, pale gums, foul breath, slight paralysis or limping, trembling or shaking, sudden weight loss, any swelling or lumps on the body, cloudy or orange-colored urine, inability to or uncontrollable urge to urinate, rampant diarrhea, moaning or whimpering, a sticky discharge from the eyes, and any unusual slobbering or salivation. If you notice any one or a combination of these symptoms, contact your veterinarian. Many diseases can cause severe damage if not treated promptly.

Two of the most common symptoms of illness are vomiting and diarrhea. They occur commonly in dogs and do not always indicate a serious ailment. Therefore, they warrant further discussion.

Vomiting

Vomiting does not always indicate a problem. A mother with newborn puppies may instinctively regurgitate food in an attempt to feed her pups. In addition, young dogs, especially puppies, often attack their food so greedily that their natural defense mechanisms send the food back up again. This behavior disappears as they mature. Nervous dogs may also vomit whenever something bothers them.

Vomiting is only considered significant when it occurs persistently. Vomiting can be caused by internal parasites, an infection, numerous digestive ailments, and other diseases. Persistent vomiting is usually accompanied by irregular bowel movements such as diarrhea. A dog exhibiting these symptoms needs veterinary attention.

Diarrhea

An occasional soft stool is not diarrhea, although diarrhea may follow. Continued watery bowel movements, however, indicate a serious ailment. Diarrhea, like vomiting, is a symptom of nearly every canine ailment, including distemper, worms, poisoning, nervous disorders, parvovirus, and intestinal blockages.

If diarrhea occurs infrequently and your dog seems otherwise healthy, it may indicate a minor stomach or intestinal upset, or perhaps an emotional upset. You can help an occasional attack of diarrhea by regulating your dog's diet. Do not give liquids such as milk or broth in food. Substituting cooked starches such as rice and macaroni should cure simple diarrhea. If it does not clear up after a few days, take your dog to your veterinarian. If left untreated, diarrhea can lead to dehydration and depression. If you see any blood in your dog's stool, contact your veterinarian immediately.

Preventive Medicine

You can take many preventive measures to keep your dog from becoming ill. Prevention starts with a well-balanced diet. Proper hygiene, an adequate exercise program, and a satisfactory dogmaster relationship are also important. Finally, be sure to have your puppy vaccinated against common communicable diseases.

Vaccinations

Dogs are vaccinated to prevent them from contracting infectious diseases. These diseases are usually caused by bacteria or viruses and can spread rapidly throughout the dog population. Vaccinations do not always guarantee permanent protection, and often annual booster shots are necessary. The two types of immunity are known as passive immunity and active immunity.

A puppy receives passive immunity when it begins to feed on immune mother's milk. The puppy receives antibodies from its mother's milk. These antibodies attack many disease-producing organisms, thus protecting the puppy. In active immunization, dead or weakened pathogens are injected into a puppy's body in order to induce it to manufacture its own antibodies. The puppy's body builds up and stores these antibodies for future use.

A reputable breeder has his or her puppies vaccinated before selling them, and should supply you with a record of this. It takes three or four weeks for an immunization to become fully effective. Your veterinarian should keep a record of all your dog's immunizations. (You will need this record if you plan to travel abroad with your dog). These records remind your veterinarian of the need for booster shots.

Preventing Infectious Diseases

Canine Distemper With the exception of rabies, canine distemper was once the most dangerous known dog disease. A highly contagious virus, it is spread through the urine, feces, saliva, and even nasal discharge of the infected animal. The virus may also be carried on blankets, brushes, and clothing. Now, however, dogs vaccinated against distemper will not contract the disease easily.

If the puppy's mother was properly vaccinated against distemper, she is able to passively immunize her newborn puppies. Such immunization lasts through nursing. After weaning, the puppies will need additional vaccinations. Bear in mind that canine distemper is very dangerous and can be very difficult to treat. Thus, vaccinating your dog is extremely important.

Early symptoms of distemper include high fever, diarrhea, dry cough, depression, and watery discharge from the eyes and nose. Advanced symptoms may include cramps, loss of equilibrium, twitching of leg and facial muscles, partial paralysis, and convulsive seizures. Vaccinations and booster shots are the only effective protection against this disease. Canine distemper is almost always fatal to a young dog that has not been

immunized. In older dogs the disease often causes nerve damage.

Canine Hepatitis This disease should not be confused with human hepatitis. Canine hepatitis is caused by a virus that primarily attacks the liver and gastro-intestinal tract. Dogs contract this virus in much the same manner as they do canine distemper. Although humans may carry the virus on their clothing, they cannot catch it. Vaccinated dogs rarely contract this disease. Canine hepatitis is almost always fatal to an unvaccinated puppy, however. Veterinarians can sometimes save an adult dog.

The symptoms of canine hepatitis include high fever, diarrhea, inflammation of the nasal passages, severe thirst, listlessness, and liver inflammation that makes the abdomen sensitive to the touch. Dogs with canine hepatitis also tend to arch their backs and rub their bellies on the floor in an attempt to relieve the pain in their livers and stomachs. Canine hepatitis develops very rapidly—a dog may appear healthy one day and very ill the next.

Leptospirosis Leptospirosis is caused by bacteria transmitted through the urine of rats, mice, or an infected dog. Dogs must ingest the bacteria to contract the disease, which attacks the kidneys and liver.

The symptoms of leptospirosis are very similar to those of canine distemper and canine hepatitis; however, leptospirosis usually causes a kidney infection that changes the color and odor of the urine. The urine of an infected dog has a deep yellow to orange color and a strong, offensive odor.

Leptospirosis causes a dog great pain; if not treated in its early stages, it is almost always fatal. On very rare occasions, leptospirosis has been transmitted to humans. Vaccinations against this disease are the only way to protect your dog, yourself, and your family.

Parainfluenza and Tracheobronchitis Parainfluenza refers to various viruses of the upper respiratory system. Tracheobronchitis is also known as kennel cough. Both diseases cause inflammation of the trachea and the bronchi, and both are common whenever and wherever dogs congregate. If you plan to board your dog in a kennel or an animal hospital, you should see that it is inoculated against these diseases.

Rabies Rabies is a viral infection that attacks the nervous system of all warm-blooded animals, including humans. It is usually transmitted through a bite in which the infected saliva of a rabid animal enters the victim's body. The virus can also be contracted if the saliva makes contact with an open wound.

Early symptoms of rabies include behavioral changes. An infected dog may be irritable one minute and friendly the next. Later symptoms include frequent urination and attempts to bite or eat foreign objects such as wood and stones. The dog then becomes vicious, drools excessively, and has difficulty swallowing. Finally, the dog becomes paralyzed, cannot eat or drink, and dies shortly thereafter.

Every dog should be vaccinated against rabies. Because rabies is dangerous to humans as well as dogs, the disease is considered a public health hazard. Any suspicion of rabies should be reported to public health authorities.

Parvovirus Parvovirus only began to appear in dogs a few years ago. Puppies should be vaccinated before their 14th week. The virus is carried and transmitted in much the same way as is canine distemper.

Two forms of parvovirus are known. One causes an inflammation of the heart muscles of very young puppies. Infected animals quickly collapse and die of heart failure. The more common form, parvoviral enteritis, is characterized by constant vomiting of a foamy, yellow-brown liquid and bloody, foul-smelling diarrhea. Patting the abdomen of an infected dog will cause it to wince in pain. Parvoviral enteritis occurs in dogs of all ages and results in heavy loss of fluids. This leads to severe dehydration and death within a few days.

If the disease is detected early enough, an unvaccinated dog can be saved by intense treatment with infusions and antibiotics. However, immunization against parvovirus is the best way to protect your dog.

Vaccination Schedule

Prior to Mating: If you intend to breed your female, bring her to your veterinarian prior to her "season." She can then receive any necessary booster shots and have her stool checked for worms. This will give her puppies passive immunity for about four to six weeks, provided she will nurse them.

Temporary Innoculations: Starting at four to six weeks of age, a puppy's passive immunity begins to wear off. Your veterinarian will then administer a series of temporary injections. Your puppy should receive shots against distemper, canine hepatitis, leptospirosis, parainfluenza, and parvovirus. Then every three or four weeks, until your puppy is four months old, it should receive additional temporary injections.

Annual Booster Shots: By having your dog inoculated every year, you can provide it maximum protection against these infectious diseases.

Of Worms and Worming

Roundworms are by far the most common internal parasites found in dogs. They are white, cylindrical in shape, and can grow up to 4 inches (10 cm). The adult worm embeds itself in the dog's intestinal tract to lay its eggs. The eggs are then passed through the dog's stool. If ingested by another animal, the eggs will grow into adult worms inside the host and continue the cycle. Although roundworms rarely cause serious illnesses in adult dogs, they can be fatal to a heavily infested puppy. Roundworms are frequently found in newborn puppies if their mother was infected during pregnancy.

Symptoms of roundworm infestation include irregular appetite, diarrhea, weakness, cramps, bloated belly, and in severe cases, paralysis. In addition, the dog's anus may itch, in which case it will skid its rump across the floor in an attempt to scratch it.

Tapeworms infiltrate young and adult dogs and are very tenacious. The head of this worm has

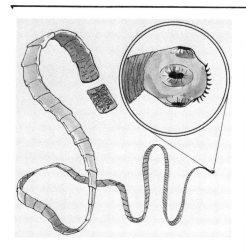

The long, segmented body of the tapeworm.
Magnification of the head reveals the hooks and suckers
it uses to attach itself to the dog's intestine.

hooks and suckers that it uses to attach itself to the
dog's small intestines. There it grows into a long
chain of segments. The tail segment contains
many eggs; occasionally the worm releases the
segments, which are passed in the dog's stool.

Symptoms of tapeworm infestation, which are
similar to those of roundworm infections, may
take a long time to develop. Tapeworms are usually diagnosed by examining the stool. Fleas are
the most common source of tapeworms, although
your golden may also get them from eating
infected, uncooked meat (especially pork and
lamb). Your veterinarian will treat tapeworms by
destroying the worm's head.

Heartworm disease is very serious and can be
fatal if not treated promptly. Heartworms are large
worms that attach themselves to the right side of
the heart and parts of the lungs. They cause the
heart to work harder and to pump blood to the
lungs. As a result, the dog's heart ages rapidly
and eventually weakens, thereby affecting all other
bodily organs.

Heartworms are transmitted by mosquitoes that
carry the worms' larvae. When the mosquito bites
a dog, the larvae can enter the dog's bloodstream.
It takes about six months for the larvae to develop
into mature worms.

You can prevent heartworms by using diethyl-
carbomozine (available from your veterinarian).
You should use this drug only if your golden has
been tested and found free of adult heartworms
because the drug can be extremely harmful to an
infested dog. Your dog should be tested annually
for heartworms prior to the mosquito season.

There are also many other forms of worms
including hookworms, kidney worms, lung-
worms, and whipworms. Each type has different
symptoms and will often require special medications. For this reason you should contact your
veterinarian promptly if you suspect your golden
is infested.

Many puppies are wormed before leaving the
breeder, and you should obtain a written record of
worming for your veterinarian. When you bring
your puppy to the veterinarian for a check-up or
for its booster shots, bring a sample of its stool in
a plastic bag. Your veterinarian will examine the
stool for evidence of infestation.

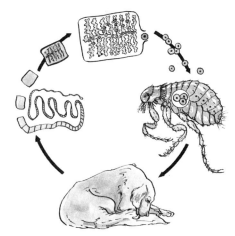

The life cycle of the dog tapeworm. Tapeworm segments
containing eggs are passed in the feces.

Ailments and Illnesses

External Parasites

Fleas are the most common canine parasite. They cause more pain and suffering to dogs than any other ailment. They differ from other parasites in that they jump, and they can jump a great distance from one dog to another. Fleas crawl under a dog's thick coat, biting and sucking its blood. This causes severe itching, and by scratching the dog may develop eczema. You may find fleas very difficult to eliminate.

Buy a flea spray or powder in your pet store. Spray or powder the entire dog, as directed on the label. Be sure to cover the dog's eyes and nose with your hand while spraying, for both sprays and powders can irritate the mucous membranes. You must also disinfect all areas where your dog may have caught the fleas, including its kennel or run, its blanket and sleeping box, and your furniture and carpets (if your dog has had any contact with them).

Lice, like all other external parasites, burrow into one area, suck blood, and cause irritation. You can see clusters of eggs on your dog's hairs if it is infested. Lice can be very dangerous, so bring your dog to your veterinarian promptly if you spot them. He or she can eliminate the lice using an insecticide dip.

Ticks are bloodsuckers which, once embedded, hang on persistently. Ticks can carry serious diseases such as Rocky Mountain Spotted Fever. Attracted by the warmth of the dog's body, ticks descend from branches and burrow into its skin.

To remove a tick, first wash the infected area with alcohol, which helps to loosen the insect's grasp. When you have loosened it somewhat, place a pair of tweezers squarely over the tick and carefully lift it off. Be careful not to pull the body apart; you must remove it whole. If the head remains under the dog's skin, it can cause an infection. Once you have removed the tick, place it in the middle of your toilet and flush.

Fleas, which can cause your golden to scratch itself almost incessantly, also serve as intermediate hosts for tapeworm.

Careful examination of your golden's skin and coat is the best method to detect external parasites such as the louse.

33

A tick, before feeding (left) and after feeding (right).

Of Mites and Mange

A dog that scratches and chews at its skin may not be suffering from flea infestation. Symptoms such as red dots, pimples, damp spots, crusty scaly skin, greasy skin, or loss of hair can mean eczema, mites, nutritional deficiencies, hormonal imbalances, allergies, and so on. Consult your veterinarian regarding the diagnosis and treatment of these ailments.

Mange, a serious skin disease, can exhibit these symptoms. Mange is caused by mites, extremely small parasites no larger than a pinhead. The two principal forms of mange are sarcoptic mange and demodectic mange. Sarcoptic mange is usually easier to recognize because it makes the dog more miserable and causes more scratching. The affected area becomes red and full of bloody sores and scabs. The skin thickens and feels leathery. The dog's hair sheds completely, leaving the affected area bare. The disease then begins to spread, and the dog produces an odor similar to that of strong cheese or that associated with a foot problem.

Demodectic mange is harder to detect because sometimes it results only in slight hair loss and some reddening and inflammation of the affected skin. Sometimes bloody pimples form that can burst and become infected. This condition does not always cause a great deal of itching or irritation. The only signs may be a small lesion about a half-inch in diameter marked by hair loss or a small bald spot.

Your veterinarian can identify either type of mange by taking skin scrapings and examining them under a microscope.

Other Skin Disorders

Additional skin disorders include allergies, eczema, and ringworm. Allergic symptoms may be similar to those of other skin ailments: inflammation, itching, pimples, flaking or scaling, and sometimes skin loss. Treatment usually takes time because your veterinarian must locate the specific cause.

Eczema is a general name for skin irritations that cannot be clearly identified. Eczema occurs in either wet or dry patches, and it may have many causes, including dietary deficiencies of Vitamin A and fat, exposure to dampness or excessive heat, hormone imbalance, and parasites.

Ringworm is not a worm but a fungus that usually attacks the outer layer of a dog's skin. It resembles mange in many respects, causing inflammation, itching, and hair loss that uncovers a scabby area. Ringworm may be carried from an infected dog to a human, so prompt veterinary treatment is essential.

Goldens were originally bred to be hunting dogs, and their prowess in the field is well known. Today, they remain one of the most popular companions of the hunter. Top left: dogs and masters in the field. Bottom left and right: retrieving the prize.

Ailments and Illnesses

Digestive Disorders

Constipation

Constipation occurs when solid waste products that cannot be easily passed build up in the dog's digestive tract. Generally, this can be relieved by changing the dog's diet and by including a mild laxative. An hourly half-cup of lukewarm milk can also be most efficacious. You should also reduce the starches in your dog's diet.

Constipation may also be caused by eating an indigestible object, such as a small toy or a stone. If you suspect this, call your veterinarian immediately. Do not give your dog a laxative if you suspect a foreign substance. This can be alleviated only by surgically removing the object.

Enteritis

Infection or inflammation of the intestine may be caused by bacteria, poisons, worms, or the swallowing of sharp objects. Regardless of the cause, any infection or inflammation of the intestinal tract is called enteritis. This condition is usually accompanied by diarrhea or foul-smelling stools. Enteritis may cause the dog much discomfort, resulting in its assuming a prayer-like position when at rest. Enteritis may indicate a serious ailment such as parvovirus. Almost all intestinal ailments require professional care, so if these symptoms appear, contact your veterinarian immediately.

Tonsillitis

Tonsillitis, an inflammation of the tonsils, is usually caused by an oral infection. A dog with tonsillitis may run a high fever, refuse to eat, drool,

Puppies selected to be hunting dogs are introduced to their new vocation at an early age. Top: A good hunting dog must be willing to take to the water. Bottom: It must also learn to handle the game with a soft mouth.

and vomit frequently and violently. Your veterinarian can treat it with antibiotics; only rarely is surgery required.

Respiratory Ailments

Dogs, like people, can contract the most common respiratory ailments, including coughs, asthma, bronchitis, laryngitis, and pneumonia. It is believed that dogs do not suffer from what we call the common cold. However, they do get a similar upper-respiratory infection. The symptoms include runny nose, thin mucus discharge from the eyes, slight fever, chills, coughing, and sneezing.

Most respiratory ailments that occur in dogs are caused by bacteria. Therefore, many of these disorders have similar symptoms.

At one time pneumonia was a common killer of dogs; however, it is now treated rather successfully with antibiotics and other drugs. Pneumonia is characterized by a rough hacking cough, shallow breathing, nasal discharge, loss of appetite, and high fever.

Most respiratory ailments can be treated with antibiotics. Take your dog to your veterinarian if it shows signs of severe respiratory problems.

Eye Disorders

Several eye disorders are inherent to the golden retriever. These ailments may be caused by genetic defects, although this has not yet been proven. Almost all eye disorders require corrective surgery, and all should be brought to your veterinarian's attention. Following is a description of several eye ailments of which you should be aware.

Trichiasis is a general term for any condition that brings eyelashes into direct contact with the cornea. This may be caused by a spastic unrolling of the eyelids or by the rubbing of an ingrown eyelash against the eye. Trichiasis causes frequent

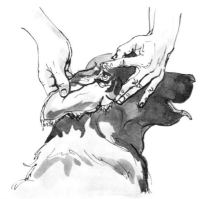

Although you can easily check your golden's outer ear for parasites, leave checking and cleaning the inner ear to your veterinarian.

squinting, excessive tearing, and conjunctivitis (an inflammation of the membrane that keeps the dog's eye moist).

When cataracts are present, part of the clear lens of the eye becomes opaque, resulting in either partial or complete loss of sight. Cataracts cause the eye to turn china blue or gray.

Progressive retinal atrophy (PRA) is a hereditary ailment that progresses for months or even years; it always leads to blindness. Therefore, make sure your golden's pedigree is free of PRA.

Other eye ailments are found in the golden retriever; however, most have no visible symptoms and can be diagnosed only by an ocular examination.

Ear Ailments

Thanks to their floppy ears, golden retrievers suffer from few ear ailments. If you suspect an ear problem, leave the dog's ear alone and contact your veterinarian. An inexperienced owner who probes too far into the sensitive ear canal can cause the dog additional damage.

Symptoms of ear disorders include persistent shaking of the head, rubbing of the ears with paws or on the floor, cocking of the head at an unusual angle, and any type of discharge from the ear. Often, the dog's ears appear reddish and inflamed.

Other Disorders

Hip Dysplasia
Hip dysplasia is a developmental abnormality resulting in an improper fit of the ball-like end of the thigh and the socket portion of the hip. This disorder is believed to be partially inherited; larger breeds like the golden retriever seem to be particularly susceptible.

At birth, the hip of a dog with severe hip dysplasia appears normal; signs of the disorder do not appear until the dog is five months or older. The optimum age for a definite diagnosis is between 24 and 36 months. Hip dysplasia results in painful inflammation of the hip joint, which leads to permanent physical damage, including lameness and the loss of the use of the back legs.

It is now possible for veterinarians to surgically alter the shape of the hip socket to assure a better fit. In addition, another surgical procedure, known as total hip replacement, has been enormously successful. Unfortunately, these procedures are performed only by a limited number of specialists, and they can be quite costly. Thus, it is extremely important to select a dog from a trouble-free bloodline.

False Pregnancy
False pregnancies are caused by imbalances in the hormone levels, which control the functions of the reproductive organs. In most cases, false pregnancies do not present physical danger, although the accompanying behavioral changes can create problems.

A female behaves very similarly during a false pregnancy as she would during a real one. She creeps off by herself, runs around restlessly, and paws at her bed. She also tends to carry toys, stuffed animals, or an old shoe to her bed, and defends them as if they were puppies. The biggest problem is that sometimes she may become overly aggressive in protecting her "offspring."

Usually this condition disappears by itself, and the female returns to normal behavior. If it occurs several times a year, take your female to your veterinarian. Although hormone therapy relieves the signs of false pregnancy, it is rarely recommended because it may cause further complications.

Your veterinarian may suggest the surgical removal of the ovaries. This is safe and will save your female a great deal of pain and may even prolong her life. Removal of the ovaries also prevents recurrence of the condition, which can lead to uterine infections. This procedure should not be performed while the symptoms of false pregnancy are still apparent, however, because the protective behavior may persist. Postpone surgery until all symptoms have disappeared.

Shock

Shock is a serious condition that results from a traumatic or emotional experience. The most common cause is an automobile accident. A dog in shock may appear asleep, or it may be semi-conscious. Symptoms vary according to the severity of the condition. Breathing may be shallow, the dog's body may be cold, and its pulse may be rapid.

If your dog is in shock, try to calm it in a soft voice, pet it reassuringly, and if possible, cover it with a blanket or an article of clothing. Because the actions of a dog in shock are unpredictable, use caution in handling it. Take it to a veterinarian immediately.

Broken bones also frequently result from automobile accidents. A dog with a fracture will be in severe pain. Therefore, always remember to approach an injured dog very carefully, as it may attempt to bite you. If a dog has a compound fracture (one in which the broken bone punctures the skin) cover the wound with gauze or a clean cloth to help prevent infections. Your veterinarian will treat the fracture either by using a splint or by pinning the bone together.

Poisoning

Although this section contains general information on poisoning, it is important for you to call directory assistance now and obtain the telephone number of the nearest poison control center. Keep this number easily accessible in case of emergency. If you know or suspect that your dog has ingested a specific poison, call the poison control center for the proper antidote. You can then relay this information to your veterinarian. If you do not know what the dog has ingested, call your veterinarian and describe the symptoms.

Common symptoms of poisoning are stomach pains, howling, whimpering, vomiting, diarrhea, convulsions, tremors, and labored breathing. Many poisons are fatal if not treated quickly. If you know the type of poison, your veterinarian may be able to save your dog by inducing vomiting or diarrhea, by pumping its stomach, or by neutralizing the poisons with appropriate medications.

One of the most common poisons ingested by dogs is rodent poison (these are usually blood anticoagulants). Symptoms include blood in the vomit, stool and urine, and nose bleeding. Such poisoning can quickly prove fatal, and a veterinarian can help only if the dog has ingested a small amount of it.

Some pesticides are extremely poisonous to dogs, so store all pesticides away from your dog. Keep the dog away from all treated plants for at least two weeks after spraying. Pesticide poisoning results in diarrhea, cramps, shortness of breath, and dizziness.

Another common cause of poisoning is antifreeze. Dogs seem to love its taste. Although antifreeze itself is not poisonous, the dog's body converts it into several toxic substances that can lead to irreversible kidney damage and eventually death. If you see your dog drink any antifreeze, take it to your veterinarian immediately.

Bee and wasp stings can cause an irritating swelling, trembling, and circulatory failure. If your dog is stung in the throat area, swelling may result that can suffocate the dog. Bring it immediately to your veterinarian.

It is always better to have two people take a golden's temperature. One person holds the dog and calms it, while the other lifts up the tail and gently introduces the thermometer into the rectum.

Nursing a Sick Dog

You should be able to perform several procedures if your dog becomes ill. The first to learn is the proper way to hold your dog, for you may need to perform various medical procedures by yourself. This technique may also prove invaluable when grooming your golden.

Lay the dog's head in the crook of your arm and hold it firmly, leaving your other arm free. If someone else can help you, lay the dog on its side and have the other person hold onto both the front and hind legs. While you do this, be sure to talk quietly to your golden to help calm and reassure it.

The second procedure is taking your dog's temperature, for which you will need a regular rectal thermometer and a jar of petroleum jelly. Because you take the dog's temperature rectally, you may need someone to help you.

The normal body temperature of an adult golden retriever is between 99.5 and 101.5°F (37.5 to 38.5°C). The temperature is slightly higher in younger dogs and slightly lower in older ones. If your dog is placid, simply shake the mercury below 99°F, lubricate the thermometer with petroleum jelly, lift the dog's tail, and slip the thermometer in. You can remove it after two or three minutes. If your dog is restless, have someone else calm it and hold its head firmly as previously described. Then lift its tail and insert the thermometer. Wash the thermometer in *cold* water when you are done. Taking your dog's temperature enables you to determine if it has a fever or is hypothermic (a symptom of poisoning).

You should also learn to take your dog's pulse. It is best to feel the pulse on the front paw or on the inside of the thigh on the heart side. An adult golden has a pulse rate of 70 to 90 beats per minute, while in younger dogs it is slightly quicker. In a calm, healthy golden, the pulse is strong and steady. A weak pulse may indicate poisoning, while an irregular, pounding pulse is a symptom of fever or infection.

Finally, it is extremely important that a sick dog take all of its prescribed medicine. If you are lucky, your dog will readily accept any form of medicine, either straight from your hand or mixed with its food. However, if your dog does not take it willingly, you must administer it another way.

When administering a pill or capsule to your golden, you may have to force its mouth open. Exert pressure on the jaw muscles with one hand, and insert the medicine into the mouth with the other.

To ensure that your golden swallows its medicine, tilt its head upward and rub its throat in a downward direction.

Powdered medications can be mixed with water and, like liquid medications, drawn into a syringe without a needle on it. Open the lips in the back of your dog's mouth near its molars, and squirt the liquid as far back into its throat as possible.

Your dog may find pills or capsules offensive. If it refuses to take a pill by itself, put it inside some hamburger or other meat. Make sure your dog swallows all the medicine. Some dogs very cleverly hide pills in their mouths and spit them out when the owner's back is turned.

If all your efforts fail, you may have to force your dog to swallow a pill. Hold the dog's upper jaw and, exerting mild pressure, raise its head. This should cause the dog's mouth to open. Quickly place the pill on the back of its tongue, hold its mouth closed, and tilt its head upward. This will force your dog to swallow the pill.

You will almost certainly need help if you must administer a suppository. Be sure to wear a disposable plastic glove for hygienic reasons. Have your assistant hold the dog with an arm across its chest, and insert the suppository as far into the anus as possible.

Breeding Golden Retrievers

Breeding Objectives

Conscientious breeders produce and raise puppies only to improve and uphold the quality and temperament of the breed. Unscrupulous breeders, however, may breed dogs only to make quick profits on inferior litters. Because of these reckless breeders, we are beginning to see behavioral abnormalities in golden retrievers. Not only do these breeders not advance the breed, they also increase the already heartbreaking number of unwanted dogs.

Serious breeders wish to improve their dogs through selective breeding with quality dogs from other well-run kennels. Their main goal is to develop a bloodline of their own, one strong in the qualities that best exemplify the Golden Retriever Standard.

The Golden Retriever Standard is a complete written description of the perfect golden: how it should look, act, and move. Of course, no one has ever produced the perfect golden, and most likely, no one ever will. However, the Standard is the goal for which serious breeders strive. The Golden Retriever Standard was prepared by the Golden Retriever Club of America and approved by the American Kennel Club. Every breed recognized by the AKC has its own Standard by which it is judged at dog shows.

If individual breeders were to produce what they considered perfect goldens, the breed would vary widely. Without standards, each breed would quickly lose its identity. Adherence to the Standard separates conscientious breeders from unscrupulous ones who are more concerned with profits than with the quality and well-being of their puppies.

The present AKC-approved Standard for Golden Retrievers was revised and put into effect in 1982. The previous Standard had been in effect since 1963.

Characteristics of the Golden Retriever

The following descriptions are based on my interpretation of the 1982 AKC-approved Standard for Golden Retrievers. However, this is not necessarily the interpretation of dog show judges. If you plan to enter your golden in a conformation competition, obtain a copy of the Golden Retriever Standard from the AKC. Remember that if you enter your golden in a show competition, only the judges' interpretation of the Standard will decide the winners.

General Appearance

The golden retriever is a hunting dog, and it should be in good physical condition. The dog should be well muscled, and neither over- nor underweight. The golden's powerful body is sound and solidly built. The dog should have both a kindly expression and an eager, alert, self-confident manner. Because the golden thrives on human contact, it always tries to behave like a member of the family.

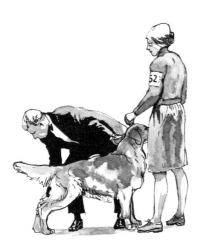

Licensed dog shows are conducted under rules established by the American Kennel Club.

Breeding Golden Retrievers

Parts of a golden retriever

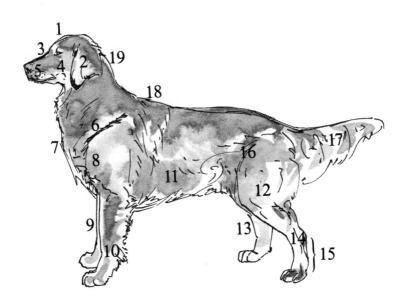

1. Skull	11. Ribcage
2. Ear	12. Stifle
3. Stop	13. Hindquarters
4. Cheeks	14. Hock
5. Muzzle	15. Rear pastern
6. Shoulder	16. Loin
7. Chest	17. Tail
8. Brisket	18. Withers
9. Forequarters	19. Neckline
10. Front pastern	

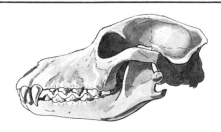

A golden should have a broad head and a muzzle that is not excessively long. In profile, the muzzle should be straight—not curved.

The Head: A golden should have a broad head and a muzzle that is not overly long. When viewed in profile, the muzzle should be straight—not curved—and blend smoothly with the skull. Although the head should appear rugged and not fragile, the face should express a soft, warm, friendly look.

The Eyes: A golden's eyes should be medium large and dark brown in color. They should be set wide apart and fairly deep into the forehead. Once again, the friendly, eager look should be reflected in the eyes.

The Teeth: The golden should have a scissor-like bite in which the outer side of the lower incisors touches the inner side of the upper incisors. It should have neither an underbite nor an overbite, nor any misalignment or gaps in the teeth.

The Nose: The nose should be black to brownish black.

The Ears: This breed should not have hound-like ears; nor should they ever appear to be sitting on top of the head. They should not be overly large, and when pulled forward, the tips should just cover the eyes. The ears (as well as the eyes) are very important features of the golden retriever's body, for they give a golden the special expression that characterizes the breed.

The Neck: A medium-length neck that gradually merges into "well laid back shoulders" gives a golden a muscular, strong, sturdy appearance.

The Body: The solid body of a golden is neither overly long nor compact. Legs that are too long or too thin make a golden appear top heavy and improperly balanced. The dog should have a deep, wide, well-developed—but not barrel-shaped—chest. It should also have a slightly sloping back, flat from the top of the shoulders to directly above the back legs.

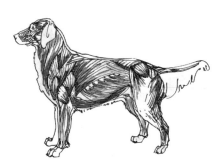

The muscular system of a golden retriever. The well-defined muscle structure results from its development as a hunting dog.

The skeletal system of the golden retriever. Note that the shoulder blades point toward the tail section, and that the stifles are well bent. This illustration also shows the flat, slightly sloped line of the golden's back.

The Forequarters: The forequarters should be muscular and should coordinate with the hindquarters when the dog moves. The shoulder blades should point toward the dog's hindquarters. This gives the dog the proper sloping back line when it stands or moves. When you view the dog from the front, the legs should appear straight and sturdy.

The Hindquarters: The golden's hindquarters must be broad and well muscled. Well-proportioned hindquarters are only slightly broader at the shoulders than at the hips. When the dog is in a natural stance, its stifles (the equivalent of human knees) should be well bent (backward to a human), and the upper leg should join the pelvis at approximately a 90 degree angle. Proper leg alignment of the hind- and forequarters helps assure proper balance and well-coordinated movement when the dog runs.

The Feet: A golden's feet are medium sized, compact, and well knuckled. The pads should be thick.

The Tail: The tail should be thick and muscular at the base. When the golden runs, the tail should curl moderately (not up over the back) and should wag. Because the tail is a key to the dog's emotional state, it should never appear between the legs.

The Coat: The coat is an important part of a hunting dog's body. It should provide protection from the elements as well as be easy to maintain. A golden's coat is naturally oily, which helps repel water. It should be firm and resilient, neither coarse nor silky. If a golden has an excessively long coat, it will be difficult to manage. It should also be fairly short, lie close to the body, and be either straight or wavy.

Color: A golden retriever should be a rich, lustrous golden. The Standard allows a wide variety of shades as long as they do not become "extremely pale or extremely dark."

The Gait: The Standard calls for a gait that "is free, smooth, powerful, and well-coordinated, showing good reach." When you view the trotting golden from any angle, the legs should be straight and turned neither in nor out. The gait should be effortless, well balanced, and coordinated.

Size: The optimum height of a male golden is 23 to 24 inches (58 – 61 cm) at the withers (the highest point of the shoulders). For a female it is 21½ to 22½ inches (55 – 57 cm). Also important is the height-to-length ratio. The length of a golden from the breastbone to the point of the buttocks should be only slightly greater than the dog's height at the withers. The dog needs this length to be able to fully extend and withdraw its limbs properly. An adult male should weight between 65 and 75 pounds (29 – 34 kg), while a female should weight between 55 and 65 pounds (25 – 29 kg).

Temperament: This is a new section of the Golden Retriever Standard, added so that breeders will consider temperament when they create new bloodlines. As previously mentioned, there has been a recent increase in the number of goldens exhibiting abnormal behavior, which must not be allowed to continue. Because temperament is one of the most important attributes of this breed, it must not be lost. Goldens must remain friendly, loving, outgoing, and trustworthy. Under normal circumstances, a golden should show no sign of either hostility or timidity.

The Standard recommends that when judging a golden retriever, more emphasis should be given to "overall appearance, balance, gait and purpose" than to individual components. When the golden's basic characteristics are analyzed, it is easy to see why this breed is an excellent choice either as a hunting dog or as a family pet.

Deviations from Breed Characteristics

As previously indicated, the Standard is a written description of the "perfect" golden retriever. Because perfect dogs do not exist, any golden judged in terms of the Standard will have "faults." Most of these are difficult to detect in a puppy; however, as the puppy grows, they become more evident.

A judge must separate winners from losers in the breeding ring. Therefore, if your golden should prove to have a major fault, do not vent your disappointment on your dog. After all, if your golden could have, it would have won just to please you. Remember that whether inside or outside the ring, *your* opinion is the only one that matters to your golden.

A fault is anything that negatively affects your golden's appearance, temperament, or movement. Timidity, hostility, nervousness, apathy, and lack of vitality and self-confidence are all undesirable traits in a golden retriever. Physical faults include a narrow head; overshot or undershot bite; low, hound-like ears; slant eyes; legs that are too long or too short; improper slope line of the back; poor color or the presence of black or white markings; and any deviation from the Standard measurements.

Remember that any of these faults apply only to bench competitions; they do not prevent the dog from competing in obedience or field competitions.

Breeding Your Golden Female

Raising puppies requires a great deal of time and space, and some hard work. It also takes a great deal of money, and rarely does it return a profit. If you wish to breed your dog or learn how to breed animals, contact an experienced breeder. A professional can help you either breed your dog or teach you the principles of dog breeding. Under no circumstances should an amateur deliberately breed his or her female.

Once you understand the principles of breeding, seek the advice of your Golden Retriever Club. They will help you find a suitable stud as well as supplying additional breeding information. Once you locate a stud, you will agree on a stud fee with the male golden's owner. Often the stud dog's owner takes the pick of the litter instead of money, but you must agree upon this ahead of time.

Choosing a Mate

After you have obtained a list of available studs from your Golden Retriever Club, you must select a dog that best complements your female. The keys to an appropriate selection are the stud's pedigree and conformation. When studying the dog's pedigree, make sure its ancestry is free of genetic problems such as hip dysplasia and eye ailments. Although breeding your female to a champion stud dog is a good start, you should place much greater emphasis on the overall quality of the dog's bloodlines.

In selecting a dog with the correct conformation, again review the Standard for Golden Retrievers. Choose a dog that best exemplifies the Standard's descriptions. Avoid a dog with faults similar to those of your female. In breeding, the objective is to improve the female's bloodline by eliminating the faults she has. Obviously, the best way to do this is to breed your female to a stud who has strong qualities wherever she has faults.

If you have difficulty selecting a stud dog, contact the breeder from whom you purchased your female. He or she can offer you invaluable assistance.

When Is the Female Ready?

Before breeding your female, wait until she is mature enough to cope with the physical and mental demands of a litter. This means waiting until she is at least 16 months old.

Prior to your female's "in season," bring her to the veterinarian to be checked for worms and for a booster shot, if she has not recently had one. Also make sure she is neither over- nor underweight.

When her season is near, check her daily for the swelling of her vulva and the appearance of color. The best time to breed a female (the time at which the chance of conception is highest) is from 9 to 14 days after the first signs of color. The female is ready for the mating when the color changes from dark red to yellow.

When the swelling and color first appear, make an appointment with the owner of the stud dog to bring the female for mating. (The female is always brought to the male.) Once mating has taken place, do not attempt to separate the dogs if they are still coupled, for this can cause injury. Once the dogs are separated, remove the female and put her in her cage or in your car. Do not allow her to urinate for about a half hour after breeding.

Remember that although your female has been bred, male dogs will still be attracted to her. Guard her carefully during the next week or so until she is definitely out of season.

The Birth of Puppies

As soon as you and your female golden return from the breeder's, begin planning for the birth of her puppies—a truly wonderful moment. After she is out of season, treat her normally and give her regular exercise. By the fifth or sixth week after mating, you should be able to tell from her body shape if she is pregnant. At this time you can change her diet to a special whelping diet—in accordance with your veterinarian's instructions. She may need more food during the seventh, eight, and ninth weeks. After about seven weeks, cut down on her exercise.

A few weeks before the puppies are due, introduce your female to either a commercial or home-made whelping box. The box must be big enough for her to lie down and stretch out, but small enough to keep the puppies from wandering away and becoming chilled. Put the box in a warm, quiet, draft-free spot, and line it with a thick layer of newspapers covered by a clean blanket and some cloths that you can easily change. Keep the temperature around the box between 70 and 80°F (21 – 27°C) for the first five weeks after the birth of the puppies. After this point they will be able to maintain their own body temperature. In the winter, you may need an additional heat source near the box, such as heat lamps. Be sure not to put the lamps either too close or too far from the box.

The gestation period of a golden retriever is usually nine weeks; your female will let you know when whelping time is near. She will become restless and wander in and out of her box. At this time, remove all distractions from around her. Only you should be present at this time. Having an audience or noisy children nearby will worry your dog. Be sure you do not disturb her. Give her plenty of room and stay nearby, speaking softly to calm her. Eventually she will settle in her box and begin her labor, which includes heavy panting followed by visible contractions. Soon the first puppy will appear at the vulva and will slide out with the contractions.

Once the pup is completely out, the mother should immediately open the amniotic sac with her teeth and shred the cord. She will begin to clean the puppy by licking it and will also massage it to stimulate its breathing. Allow her to eat the afterbirth, as this promotes the production of milk and encourages further labor for the next puppy. The others should follow in about half-hour intervals. Keep in mind that the average golden litter is eight puppies, so labor will last about seven to eight hours from the time the heavy panting starts to the birth of the last puppy. A golden mother has only ten teats. If her litter is larger than that, the additional puppies should be "wet-nursed" so that she is not overburdened.

Usually, a female gives birth without any problems; however, on rare occasions she seems to lack basic maternal instincts. If this happens, you will have to finish the delivery. First, firmly pinch the umbilical cord closed in the middle with your fingers (or with pliers, if necessary). Cut the cord a few inches from the puppy's belly with a pair of scissors. Then open the sac near the nose and remove it from around the puppy. Next, open the mouth and gently remove any mucus obstructing the breathing passages. Finally, rub a warm towel briskly back and forth across the puppy's chest for about 15 minutes to stimulate its breathing.

Care of Puppies

Although newborn puppies cannot see or hear, they do have a well-developed sense of smell that helps them locate the mother's teats. During the first few weeks, the mother takes complete care of her puppies. She nurses them, washes them, and even licks up their excreta in order to keep the whelping box clean. Be sure to change the box lining whenever necessary. Besides this, however, you will have very little to do until the puppies are almost four weeks old.

By the fourth week, the puppies' eyes are completely open, their hearing is more acute, and they are aware of their environment. You can now begin to wean them. Weaning means that the puppies stop depending on their mother for food and begin to eat on their own. Begin weaning as soon as possible, for the mother's milk supply quickly runs short of the demand.

One of the easiest ways to wean puppies is to purchase high-quality commercial puppy food from your pet store and soften it using hot water. The food should be lukewarm and of thin consistency when served to puppies. Gradually decrease the water until the puppies are eating dry food. Once they have reached this stage, begin adding small pieces of fresh meat or canned puppy food.

When feeding puppies for the first time, place them around a large, flat dish full of lukewarm puppy food. Dip your finger into the food and smear some on the end of each puppy's nose. They will use their tongues to clean their noses, and will begin eating the food.

When the puppies are about six or seven weeks old, take them to your veterinarian for a series of temporary shots. Also bring a few stool samples so the veterinarian can check for worms. Many puppies become infested with roundworms contracted from their mothers. These worms can be harmful if left untreated. If worming is needed, medicate the puppies as directed by your veterinarian.

When the puppies are old enough to begin wandering throughout your house, be sure to remove anything that may be harmful if chewed or eaten. Give the puppies something to chew in order to strengthen their jaw muscles and teeth—rawhide bones or other teething toys specifically designed for puppies.

Golden puppies are naturally curious and should not avoid human contact. If a puppy tends to be wary of humans, increase your contact time with it until it no longer fears people.

When the puppies are seven weeks old, it is

A mother golden nursing her pups. The puppies seem to have worn mom out.

time for them to leave their littermates and find new homes. Your Golden Retriever Club can advise you on finding them homes. Naturally, you will be very concerned about the quality of homes your puppies receive. Do not be afraid to ask prospective buyers about their homes and their views on dog ownership. Remember the questions asked of you when you purchased your golden. Now you can understand the breeder's concern for the puppies' well being. If you decide to keep one or more puppies, bear in mind the space, time, and money raising puppies requires.

Dog Shows and Exhibitions

A purebreed such as the golden retriever may be entered in any dog show, obedience competition, or field trial. These licensed shows are conducted under rules established by the AKC.

The term "dog show" usually refers to a bench competition in which a golden retriever is judged on appearance, physique, bearing, and temperament. At obedience trials a golden is judged entirely on performance in a series of exercises. These exercises, chosen beforehand by the AKC, are based upon any work the dog may be required to do. The exercises to be performed are based on the dog's experience in the obedience ring and may include heel on leash, heel free, recall, long sit, retrieve on flat or over high jump, broad jump, scent discrimination, or a signal exercise. Field trials, competitions designed for hunting dogs, attempt to simulate actual hunting conditions.

Because each event has a different format, you should attend them to learn more about judging. Also, these competitions offer dog owners a wide variety of helpful information. Manufacturers of dog food and other pet products often attend and sometimes display their merchandise. You will also be able to exchange tips with other dog owners and breeders. Often the judges advise owners on the care and grooming of their dogs.

If you wish to enter your dog in a show, check with your local Golden Retriever Club. They can advise you about the event, help you obtain and complete the application form, and inform you of the entry fee. Prior to the show, you must supply the judges with your dog's pedigree, certificate of health, and an International Certificate of Immunization.

Whether you enter your golden or not, attending a dog show is rewarding and educational. If you do decide to enter your dog, do not expect it to win all the accolades or to achieve a good score. Remember that dog show judges are very strict. Your golden may not meet their interpretation of the Standard. If this is the case, just enjoy the show and the experience of owning a purebreed dog.

Basic and Advanced Training

Golden retrievers truly excel in training. Because they love human companionship, you can begin training them much earlier than many other breeds. In addition, if you conduct your training program properly, you will be able to keep your golden puppy's attention for a longer period, thus leading to quicker learning.

Even if you do not plan to enter your dog in field or obedience trials, you should still teach it the skills for which it was developed. This includes any of the retrieving and hurdling exercises.

Bear in mind that this chapter does not describe all the skills a golden can learn. In fact, I believe that if you have the time, patience, and energy, you can teach your golden an endless number of skills. You must, however, be able to communicate your ideas to your eager student.

Because they learn rapidly, if taught properly goldens are extremely obedient. Goldens, along with German shepherds and Labrador Retrievers, dominate the guide dog (Seeing-Eye) field. This trainability has made the golden retriever one of the top breeds competing in field and obedience trials.

Why Dogs Learn

Dogs are instinctively pack animals. Because they hunt and live as a group, dogs must learn to co-exist with each other in order to survive. This co-existence depends on ranking order. Each dog has a place in the ranking order, usually based on strength and experience. In the pack, all dogs submit to a dog of higher authority. Similarly, a domesticated dog submits only to a higher ranking authority.

Through training a puppy learns that you are its master and that the other members of your family rank higher than it does. In addition to establishing ranking order, training teaches your puppy the rules of your house. Teaching a puppy actions and behaviors that are not instinctive takes patience, understanding, and love. You must be consistent and authoritative, yet must never lose your temper. Try to understand that human ways are unfamiliar to your golden puppy, but that it is eager to learn. Your puppy depends on you to find the proper way to teach it. Once you find the right method, your puppy will respond eagerly and joyfully.

Basic Rules of Training

Each time you hold a training session for your golden, consider the following points:

1) You and your family must be consistent. All household members must decide what is permitted and what is prohibited. Once you have taught your dog a lesson, never allow it to do the contrary without reprimand.

2) Be authoritative. Although your dog must learn that you are in charge, *never* do this by using physical force. Goldens can quickly learn hand signals, and they can understand sounds. Therefore, make all visual and verbal commands clearly and unambiguously. Because dogs understand tones better than words, be sure your reprimands are always sharp and firm while your praise is always calm and friendly.

3) Run each training session with an atmosphere conducive to learning. Have your dog perform the lesson where there are as few distractions as possible. In addition, never attempt to teach a puppy anything if you are in a bad mood. This will only confuse the puppy and make learning harder.

4) Do not attempt to teach your dog more than one concept in a single training session, and never move on to another concept until your dog has mastered the previous lesson. Puppies, like people, learn at their own pace and should never be rushed.

5) Praise your dog thoroughly after it has performed correctly. Verbal praise and petting or scratching behind the ears will make your golden an eager learner. Goldens never need food rewards. Your puppy must learn to perform correctly whether or not you reward it.

6) Punish disobedience immediately. Because a

puppy has a very short memory, never hesitate to reprimand it. If your puppy chews your slipper (which you should remember not to leave within its reach), do not punish it unless you catch it in the act. You should certainly reprimand an adult dog that knows better after showing it the slipper, providing it leaves a shred of evidence. Punishment should take the form of verbal disapproval. In extreme conditions you may place the dog in its cage after verbally reprimanding it.

7) Begin working with your puppy the day you bring it home. Hold two or three sessions a day, and continue these sessions as long as your puppy shows interest. By limiting your sessions to 10 or 15 minutes each, you will provide sufficient teaching without boring your dog. Your puppy may need two weeks or longer to begin to understand some of your commands, so do not neglect your training. Goldens must learn these basic lessons at a young age.

Training a Puppy

As previously mentioned, training begins the day you bring your puppy home. The longer you wait, the more difficult it will be for your puppy to learn. First teach your golden its name. If you always address your puppy using its name, you will be amazed at how fast it will learn this lesson. Make sure your golden does not hear nicknames; this will confuse it, and it will not respond when called.

Another important lesson is the meaning of "no." Your puppy will probably have to begin learning this lesson its first day at home. As your puppy first explores your home, it will probably do something wrong. When it does, tell it "no" in a sharp, firm tone that shows you are serious. If your puppy refuses to listen, pick it up and place it in its cage. *Never* hit your puppy, either with your hand or with a rolled newspaper, for this will make your puppy hand-shy. Using a cage will simplify training. In addition, as you will see in the next section, it will also speed the process of housebreaking.

Housebreaking

Many people choose an older dog rather than a puppy because they think housebreaking a puppy is too difficult. This may be true if you paper train your puppy. However, paper training is not recommended for large breeds. Using a wire cage is much easier and faster. The cage becomes the puppy's "house," and—fortunately for humans—dogs instinctively need to keep their houses clean.

When the puppy first encounters the cage, it may be wary. To make it feel more comfortable, feed it or give it a toy to play with inside the cage. After you have confined your puppy to its cage a few times with its excreta, it will quickly learn to "hold it in" until you let it out of the cage. This means that after you take the puppy out of its cage, bring it outdoors immediately. Establish a time schedule for taking your puppy out of its cage. Wait for it to relieve itself before bringing it back indoors. As your trust in your puppy grows, you can let it out for longer and longer periods, until eventually you can leave the cage door open at all times, provided you take the dog outside as scheduled.

Some people feel that confining a dog to a cage is cruel. Let me assure you that it is not. Your dog will actually prefer the security of its cage, and once it is accustomed to sleeping there, it will return there on its own. Remember that if the dog did not enjoy the cage, it would never go in voluntarily. If you decide to use a cage, you can also use it as a sleeping box. In addition to offering safety and comfort, the cage is useful when you are unable to supervise your puppy.

If you cannot bear to use a cage, however, you do have an alternative for housebreaking. Take your puppy outdoors after every meal so it can relieve itself. Once outside, your puppy may sniff and explore for a long while before it defecates and urinates. Remain patient and allow your puppy to take its time. Take the dog out every two to three hours.

Regardless of the housebreaking method you choose, always take your dog for its last walk as late at night as possible. In addition, you can tie your golden to its bed. This may help your dog wait until its morning walk to relieve itself.

Accidents will happen no matter how you choose to housebreak your golden. Never spank your puppy or put its nose in the mess. This serves no purpose and only upsets the puppy. Instead, scold the dog with a sharp "No!" Then put it in its cage if you are using one. If you do not catch the dog either in the act or shortly afterward, punishing it will do no good at all. Because puppies have very short memories, a delayed scolding will only confuse it.

Walking on a Leash

From the very first time you walk your puppy, begin to teach it how to walk on a leash. Place a collar on the puppy, making sure it is neither too tight nor too loose. Attach a leash and take your puppy for its first walk. Teach your puppy to walk on your left side. Try to keep it close to your leg, but not under your feet, and do not allow it to pull you along. Remember to be patient. If your puppy falls behind, do not attempt to drag it behind you. Keep it in its proper walking position with friendly words and a little gentle force, if necessary.

Begging Is Forbidden

Begging is a bad habit for a puppy to develop. Do not allow it to begin. If, when you sit down for a meal, your puppy starts to beg or just sits nearby, staring at you with pleading eyes, be firm. Say in a strict tone, "No!" and point away from the table and toward the puppy's cage or sleeping box. Within a few weeks your puppy will learn not to approach the table at mealtime.

Being Alone

A puppy must learn early that it will be left alone on occasion. You must teach it to behave properly while you are away, for a poorly trained golden puppy can cause a great deal of damage.

To accustom your puppy to being alone, leave it in a familiar room. Then go into another room

where the puppy can neither see nor hear you. Stay there for a short while and then return; if your puppy has done anything wrong, reprimand it. Gradually increase the time you leave the dog in the room.

If you must leave before you can trust your puppy alone, lock it in its cage with food, water, and toys until you return. If you do not have a cage, lock it in a familiar room. Remove all tempting objects, including shoes, papers, and clothing. Make sure you leave the puppy its bed and an ample supply of food, water, and toys.

Do not leave a very young puppy alone in your yard, where there are too many uncontrollable factors. Children may tease the puppy, and other animals may be able to bother or hurt it.

Simple Commands

The first commands to teach your puppy are "sit," "stay," "come," and "heel." Teach these commands using these words and not phrases like, "Come over here, Max." Your puppy does not understand complete sentences, but rather relies on the command word, your tone, and your gestures. Do not try to teach your puppy these commands for long periods of time. It is better to train for short periods two or three times a day. Train your puppy before you feed it because afterwards it may be sluggish. Also, make sure to walk the dog before training. To avoid distractions, train your puppy in a confined area without an audience.

These are all familiar scenes to the breeder. Top left: A future mother awaiting new arrivals. Top right: Nursing puppies. (Note the appropriate size of the whelping box.) Bottom left: Older puppies that are ready to be weaned. Bottom right: Puppies eating on their own.

Basic and Advanced Training

The simple command "Sit." You can help your golden learn by pushing gently on its hindquarters while keeping its head up with the leash.

Sit: Take your puppy into an isolated room and fit it with a collar and leash. Hold the leash with your right hand and place your left hand on the puppy's hindquarters. Then give the command "Sit!" or "Sit Max!" in a firm voice, at the same time pressing gently and steadily on its hindquarters. Gently pull the leash upward to keep your puppy from lying down on the floor. Hold the dog in this position for a while. Do not allow it to jump back up.

Do not expect your golden to master this command after the first training session. Repeat the procedure for the entire session or until the puppy begins to lose interest. Remember to praise its efforts each time it sits properly. If you repeat the procedure every day, your golden will quickly learn this command.

Once your puppy has performed the sit at least a couple of times in succession, remove the leash. If your dog has been properly trained, it will perform correctly. If not, remain patient and try again with the leash on.

If you want to use your golden in the field, teach it to respond to a hand signal as well. In the field your dog may be at a distance where it can see you but not hear you. This way your dog can understand your command even if noise prevents it from hearing you. Once your puppy has mastered the command, hold up either your hand or a single finger in a distinct gesture and say "Sit," making sure the dog can see the signal. Always use the word and the gesture together so your dog connects the two.

Stay: This is a more difficult command to teach your golden, for it will always want to be at your side. The "Stay" command orders your dog to remain still wherever it is. This command may someday save your dog's life.

Puppies quickly learn to respond attentively to their master's voice—with or without the example of an obedient dam.

The "Stay" command. Using the hand gesture while speaking the verbal command accelerates the learning process.

In teaching your dog to "stay," first fit it with a leash and collar. Then run through the "Sit" procedure and follow it with the command "Stay." As you say this new command, raise your hand, palm toward the dog, like a police officer stopping traffic. Each time your dog attempts to stand up, reproach it with a sharp "no!"

Take up all the slack in the leash to hold your dog in place. Repeat the procedure until the dog appears to understand. Then remove the leash and repeat the command several times. Praise the dog each time it obeys. If it disobeys, reprimand it.

Once you have repeated this command with regular success, begin to back away from the dog slowly, always maintaining eye contact. As you back away, keep repeating the word "Stay" while making the proper hand gesture. If your dog attempts to follow you, give it a loud, sharp "Stay!" If it continues to follow you, reprimand it. If the dog stays when told, praise it greatly, for it will be very tempted to follow you.

Come: If you call your golden puppy's name, it will probably barrel across the room to greet you. However, your dog may eventually find something that attracts its attention more than you. The objective of the command "Come" is to have your dog come running whether it wants to or not.

You should teach the command "Come" to your puppy right after "Sit" and "Stay." Start by running through the "Sit" and "Stay" procedures. Once it has "stayed" at a good distance, call it by name and follow with the command, "Max, come!" Accompany your words with a lively sound or gesture like clapping your hands or slapping your thighs. This will help excite your dog into motion.

Your golden will quickly associate the word "Come" with your movements. Praise it for responding correctly. If it does not respond to the command, put it on a long rope and let it wander off. Then slowly reel in the rope while repeating the word "Come." Shower your dog with praise when it reaches you. Repeat this exercise several times; then try it without the rope again. "Come" is another command that can protect your dog from dangerous situations.

When you begin to teach your golden the "Heel" command, use a shortened grasp on the leash and keep the dog's head level with your knee.

Training for the Obedience Ring

The golden retriever has been a dominant force in the obedience ring for years. The exercises described in this section are important for your dog to learn if you plan to enter it in obedience competitions. However, exercises such as "heeling" or "relinquishing an object" are valuable for any dog to learn. Both will help reinforce your dog's understanding of his subordination to you.

Using Obedience Schools for Training

Obedience schools are not schools for "wayward" dogs, but rather places where your dog can learn all the exercises it must know to compete in shows. Even if you do not plan to enter your dog in a show, obedience schools offer an enjoyable, interesting, easy alternative to training your dog alone. At these schools you will work under the guidance of an experienced dog handler.

If you have an older child, let him or her take your golden to obedience classes. This allows child and dog to spend more time together. It also teaches your child how to care for a dog responsibly. Working with a dog at obedience school will teach your child greater respect for both the dog and him- or herself.

Check with your Golden Retriever Club and the AKC for a reputable obedience school in your area. Before enrolling your dog, make sure the class suits your purpose. Most schools offer special classes for owners interested in showing their dogs, and others for amateurs. Remember that obedience school can be costly, depending on the courses you choose and the problems your dog presents.

Heeling

When a dog "heels," it walks at your left side with its head level with your knees. Your golden should learn to "heel" first on a leash, and eventually to walk correctly without restraint.

To start, run through the commands your dog has already mastered. This will give your dog confidence before starting this difficult lesson. Firmly grasp your dog's leash with your left hand about halfway toward its collar, enabling you to guide it. Walk briskly and give the command "Heel!" or "Heel, Max!" in a sharp tone of voice. At first your dog will probably act unpredictably. It may bolt ahead, pull back, or even jump about in an effort to play.

If your dog lags behind, pull steadily on the leash to bring it even with your leg. Do not drag the dog forward or force it to obey your commands, for this will destroy your well-established learning atmosphere. If your dog runs forward, pull it back to your side and give the "Heel" command again. If you have difficulty getting your dog to perform correctly, run it through the old "Sit" and "Stay" exercises. Whenever your dog responds correctly, praise it. When it reacts improperly, reprimand it immediately. When it has performed the "Sit" and "Stay" correctly, begin the "Heel" exercises again.

Do not try to teach your dog to heel too quickly. This lesson usually takes a long time and much patience. Once your dog has mastered the heel on

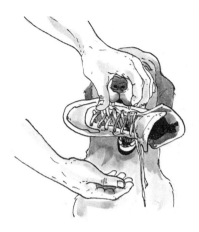

Sometimes you will need gentle force when teaching your golden to release an object.

the leash, take it through a turning exercise. If it has trouble heeling while you turn, take a shorter grip on the leash to persuade it to turn as you do. As you do this, repeat the command "Heel" in a sharp tone. Once your dog begins to learn, walk it through a series of straight line, right turn, and left turn exercises. When it has mastered turning, begin training on a slack leash.

Go through the heeling exercises with the leash exerting no pressure on your dog's collar. At the dog's first mistake, grasp the leash firmly and lead the dog steadily in the proper direction. When it performs correctly, remember to praise it.

When your dog has learned to walk correctly with a slack leash, remove the leash completely. If it has performed properly with a loose leash, you should achieve similar results after removing the leash. If your dog reverts to bad habits, immediately reprimand it with a sharp "no!" If necessary, put the leash back on. Then run through the "Heel" lessons and try again without the leash. It is very important to remember to praise your dog whenever it performs an exercise properly to reinforce its good behavior.

Basic and Advanced Training

Relinquishing an Object

This is usually easy for golden retrievers to learn, for they are not as possessive as some other breeds. Start by giving your dog a ball or a suitably sized piece of non-splintering wood to hold in its teeth. Then command the dog to sit, praising it once it obeys the command. Slowly pull the dog's jaws apart with both hands and say, "Let go!" strictly and firmly. If it begins to growl, tell it "no!" Do not be afraid if your dog growls, for this is its natural reaction to anyone who attempts to take away its prey. Rarely will a golden do more than growl.

Lying Down

Start by having your dog sit. Then slowly pull its front legs forward, push down on its shoulders, and command it firmly by saying "Down." Carefully step on the leash to prevent the dog from returning to its feet. Keep the dog in this position for about one minute. Gradually increase the time period as your dog progresses. When your dog begins to lie down on its own, begin to walk away from it while maintaining constant eye contact. Whenever the dog attempts to stand up, repeat the command "Down" in a firm, sharp tone.

Retrieving

Retrieving will obviously come fairly naturally to a golden. Simply throw a stick or a ball, with your dog standing next to you, and call out "Fetch." Your golden will probably go after the object and return it to you. Command the dog to sit, put out your hand, palm up, under its lower jaw, and say, "Let go!" You should be able to remove the object from the dog's mouth without any resistance. If your dog drops the object on the ground, place it back into its mouth, and then remove it, saying "Let go!" If your golden shows no desire to return with the object, repeat the exercise using a 30-foot (9 m) rope. Tie the dog to the cord, throw the object, and call out "Fetch!" again. Once it has picked up the object, draw the dog toward you. Then take the object from it.

Jumping over Hurdles

Because goldens truly enjoy jumping, they learn this lesson with relative ease. First, command your dog to sit on one side of a small pile of boards, while you stand on the opposite side. Command the dog by saying "Jump!" If it walks around the obstacle, say "no!" then bring it back and start over. Praise your dog for a successful performance.

As your dog learns to jump over the hurdle on command, gradually increase the obstacle's height. Be careful not to make the jump too high, for this can hurt young dogs and discourage further jumping.

Once your dog has learned to jump on command, begin a jump and retrieve exercise. Place the object to be retrieved on the other side of the hurdle. Command your dog to sit next to you. Then command it to retrieve the object by saying, "Jump! Fetch!" in a clear, firm voice. The dog should leap over the obstacle, pick up the object, and jump back with it. Tell the dog to sit again. Then take the object out of its mouth by saying, "Let go!" Praise your dog warmly for its accomplishments.

As their name implies, goldens love to retrieve objects—in this case a wooden dumbell.

Problems in Training

Remember that all golden retrievers are different. Each has its idiosyncrasies, and learning abilities vary greatly. I have found that more than half the battle is establishing the proper rapport with your dog. All the training exercises described in this chapter are no more than outlines for teaching commands. As your dog's trainer, you must establish an appropriate communication system in which your dog will understand what you want it to perform.

If your dog shows an unwillingness to learn a lesson, remain calm and understanding. Never force your golden to learn. Anger and beatings have *never* helped a dog learn anything. Such actions only create an atmosphere inconducive to learning, and cause your dog to lose its trust in you.

If your dog does not seem to be learning a particular lesson, examine your teaching methods. Review the section on basic rules of training and review each of the seven points listed. Ask yourself if you have followed these points during all of your training sessions.

In most cases, the fault lies in the owner's teaching methods. If you feel, however, that this is not the problem, then carefully examine your dog and its environment. Are you holding your lessons where your dog is being distracted by an outside force, or is your dog ill? If you suspect illness, bring your dog to your veterinarian.

If you continue to have difficulty training your dog, contact your Golden Retriever Club and/or a highly recommended obedience school. These facilities have professional dog handlers who can examine your training regimen and help you iden tify problems.

If you are diligent and establish a harmonious learning atmosphere for your dog, you and your faithful, four-legged friend will enjoy many wonderful years of camaraderie.

Field Trials

As previously mentioned, a field trial is a competition designed to resemble actual hunting conditions. In a field trial, dogs must retrieve fallen game. In addition to being judged on retrieving ability and control, the golden must battle such obstacles as heavy woods, dense thickets, and water.

You cannot train your dog for a field trial alone. Training a dog for this type of competition requires a great deal of dedication and time. These trials are expensive as well as fiercely competitive. These trials become a way of life for the participants. Field trialers have relationships with their dogs that are rarely equaled by other dog owners. To learn more about field trials, contact the Golden Retriever Club of America.

Guide Dog Training

By now you know that goldens are friendly, obedient, patient, and easy to train. In addition to these qualities, their body size and almost maintenance-free coat make them ideal guide dogs. Goldens chosen to be trained as Seeing-Eye dogs are selected by experts who determine that the dogs have all necessary qualifications.

All guide dogs must be trustworthy and friendly to all people (the dog must be able to guide its master through crowds), patient, and totally obedient. Guide dogs usually begin their training at the age of one year. They undergo much more vigorous training than goldens that compete in the obedience ring. Guide dogs must learn that there is no room for error, for mistakes can mean serious harm to their masters.

There are basic differences between guide dog and regular training. Guide dogs are trained to take the lead and to show initiative, while all other dogs are taught to follow their masters. Guide dogs must learn to work with a harness. Also, guide dogs must learn to avoid obstacles, while ring dogs must learn to hurdle them.

Although all golden retrievers possess many of the requirements needed to be guide dogs, not all of them have all the necessary physical, temperamental, and mental characteristics. Only exceptionally talented dogs are chosen for this duty.

Understanding the Golden Retriever

Origins and Early History

The development of the golden retriever began in the 19th century with the very careful planning and dedication of an Englishman, Sir Dudley Marjoriebanks, the first Lord of Tweedmouth. Lord Tweedmouth lived on an estate in Scotland, where he did a great deal of hunting. His fondness for hunting led him to search for the perfect hunting dog. He attempted to reach his goal by obtaining good hunting dogs that he then outcrossed with other breeds. Outcrossing is a process by which dogs with no mutual ancestors are bred together. The purpose is to continue the special hunting traits of different breeds. Through outcrossing, Sir Dudley eventually developed a breed later known as the golden retriever.

The golden retriever was originally believed to have been the result of the crossbreeding of Russian tracking dogs and bloodhounds. This was still believed in the early 1950s. In 1952, however, the original Stud Book of Lord Tweedmouth was made available for study by his great nephew, the sixth Earl of Ilchester. The Stud Book was a detailed record of all Lord Tweedmouth's breeding attempts in the mid- to late 19th century.

Lord Tweedmouth purchased a yellow retriever from a cobbler in Brighton in 1865. The dog, named Nous, was the only yellow in a litter of black, wavy-coated retrievers. Black wavy-coats, the predecessors of today's flat-coated retrievers, were developed from crosses of lesser Newfoundlands and several types of setters. Lesser Newfoundlands were an early American breed and should not be confused with present-day Newfoundlands.

The female bred with Nous was a tweed water spaniel named Belle. This breed is now extinct, and its exact origins are unknown. We do know, however, that early water spaniels were a cross between various spaniels and early water dogs. Water spaniels were known for their superior retrieving abilities, high intelligence, and excellent swimming skills.

The litter of Nous and Belle consisted of four females—Ada, Primrose, Crocus, and Cowslip.

Although all were very important to Lord Tweedmouth, records indicate that Cowslip had the greatest number of traits that he deemed desirable for the development of the perfect hunting retriever.

Lord Tweedmouth's plan was to carefully line-breed all his dogs back to Cowslip. Linebreeding means breeding a female to a dog that has the same ancestors (although it is not directly related). First, Lord Tweedmouth obtained another tweed water spaniel and bred it to Cowslip. From this litter, he took a female puppy and later bred her to a descendant of Ada. He performed this type of linebreeding for several generations. In order to reduce the risks of excessive linebreeding, however, he made several outcrosses. He introduced black, wavy-coated retrievers to the line in order to improve hunting abilities. He added an Irish setter—another hunting dog—in order to improve the breed's color. Finally, he used a sandy-colored bloodhound to increase tracking ability and to insure color.

Today's golden retriever is the result of very selective linebreeding for type and planned outcrossing for ability and color. Lord Tweedmouth's dedicated work produced the original line of golden retrievers, the Ilchesters. In 1903, the Kennel Club of England first registered the golden retriever under the category "Flat-Coats-Golden." In 1911, the Kennel Club recognized goldens as a separate breed called "yellow or golden retrievers." A few years later "yellow" was dropped from the name, and the Lord of Tweedmouth's breed became known officially as the golden retriever.

The Golden Retriever in the United States

The archives of the Golden Retriever Club of America (GRCA) record goldens in the United States as early as the 1890s. However, no serious breeding was documented until the 1930s. In 1933, Colonel Samuel Magoffin showed a golden import named Speedwell Pluto. That year the dog won Best In Show at Puget Sound, Washington, the first time a golden won this honor in the United States.

The AKC officially recognized the golden retriever in 1932, although registrations of the breed had been accepted earlier. In 1938, the Golden Retriever Club of America was formed; its first president was Colonel Magoffin. Today the GRCA is one of the largest parent breed clubs in the United States. Its purpose is to advance and protect the golden in all aspects of life—whether as show dog, hunting dog, or family companion. If you are interested in goldens, by all means join the GRCA. It will prove a valuable source of help and information regarding nearly all your dog's needs.

The Nature of the Golden Retriever

Now that we have examined the origins of the golden, you can see how it acquired its size, shape, and color. To understand the golden's behavior patterns, however, we must examine the process by which dogs evolved and were domesticated. All dogs, regardless of breed, trace their ancestry to a form of wild dog or wolf.

As previously mentioned, wild dogs have a specially structured society. Most of their behavior rituals allow each member of the pack to live in harmony with the others. With the passing of many, many generations of dogs, some of these rituals became instinctive. Modern domesticated dogs will exhibit many of these instinctive behavior patterns, including marking of territory and establishing a ranking order among human companions.

Compared with most other breeds, the golden retriever appears not to possess as many instinctive behavior patterns. For example, goldens rarely exhibit such survival instincts as fighting spirit, possessiveness over food, or the urge to protect its home or itself. The golden may mark its territory; however, it will not defend it with the zeal of a German shepherd, for example.

It is believed that dogs were the first domesticated animal; evidence indicates that this process began about 12,000 years ago. Humans probably tamed wolves or wild dogs to assist them in hunting. Hunting practices and social structures of both humans and dogs were probably very similar at this time.

As dogs became domestic, they lost many of their instinctive behavior patterns but retained others. Which traits were lost and which were retained depends on the specific breed and how it was domesticated. As you know, golden retrievers were originally bred as hunting dogs, as were all their domestic ancestors. Thus, goldens naturally display excellent hunting and tracking skills.

Because goldens and their domestic ancestors were all hunting dogs, they received a great deal of human contact. Dogs used as retrievers must undergo substantial training by a hunter. This relationship turns the dog into a companion as well as a hunting tool. More than any other factor, this training is probably responsible for the people-oriented nature of the golden retriever.

The gentle, friendly, obedient nature of the golden retriever is the result of generations of selective breeding. Since the mid-19th century, breeders have carefully developed the traits they deemed desirable in goldens and have tried to eliminate unwanted behavior patterns. Thus, breeders have successfully weeded out many inherent canine behaviors that would be undesirable in hunting dogs.

In summary, the nature of the golden retriever is a blend of three elements. The first includes all instinctive behavior, such as sexual drive, the marking of territories, and the establishment of a ranking order. The second and third elements are a result of domestication; they include selectively bred traits and "people-oriented" traits developed from the hunger-dog relationship.

Golden Retrievers are rapid learners and can quickly be taught many simple commands. Top left: "Stay." Top right: "Come." Bottom left: "Heel" (without a leash). Bottom right: Under the proper conditions, goldens can also learn numerous tricks including "sit up."

Behavior Problems

Although the golden retriever is renowned for ease of training as well as a friendly nature, in recent years, accounts have been told of goldens too hyperactive for average owners to properly train. An increasing number of reports have also been made regarding unprovoked attacks by goldens upon other dogs and people, including their owners. Not all of these incidents are believed to be the result of poor training. The cause of these temperament problems is probably careless breeding practices, for the golden's loving nature is the result of many years of well-planned, careful training.

Abnormal behavior patterns are practically impossible to detect in a golden puppy. Therefore, be sure to purchase your puppy from a reliable, conscientious breeder. Even if you do this, however, your dog may still develop behavioral problems. You can control most of these abnormalities by extensive training and counterconditioning. In addition, for the sake of the breed, do not breed a golden that exhibits behavior problems. You do not want to increase the incidence of these problems.

What Your Dog Can Tell You

All dogs use their voices, body language, and facial expressions to convey their emotions. Sometimes you must pay special attention to these characteristics in order to understand your dog's moods.

Dogs do not make noises without a reason. Each sound reflects a mood. A dog will yelp in fright or pain, whine and whimper in loneliness or when seeking attention, groan in contentment or when ailing, and bark in anger or glee. Often you must look for additional signs to determine the purpose of the sounds.

As their name indicates, goldens are naturals at retrieving. Give a golden a stick to fetch and it will be your friend for life. The golden, left, is combining retrieving with another favorite activity, swimming.

Body language is also a good indicator of a dog's mood. A joyous dog jumps up and down eagerly and may bark. A dog that crouches and lowers its head to the floor is exhibiting fear, either of being punished or of an intruder or another dog. The best indicator of your dog's emotions, however, is its tail. A happy dog wags its tail briskly (the happier it is, the more briskly its tail wags). A frightened dog puts its tail between its legs. An alert or attentive golden raises its tail slightly, while a content dog has a lowered tail (but not between its legs).

Finally, watch your golden's ears and muzzle, for they are a primary means of facial expression. A content golden has a closed mouth and lowered ears. An alert, aroused, or attentive dog picks up its ears (only the part of the ear on the top of the golden's head rises, not its entire ear). Often your dog will cock its head inquisitively to one side or the other. Be wary of *any* dog whose ears are back, upper lips are raised, mouth is open, and is growling. Although you will rarely—if ever—see a golden retriever in this position, remember that these are all warning signals of fear and/or anger, and they may precede an attack.

The Sense Organs

Dogs in general rely heavily on the senses of smell, hearing, taste, and touch, and less on the sense of sight. Like other traits, sense organs in a particular breed have been developed through selective breeding and domestication.

The sense of smell is very important to a golden. This sense enables them to find food and mates, and to decipher territories. Because goldens have long been bred as hunting dogs, their highly developed sense of smell enables them to track game expertly.

The area of the olfactory system concerned with smell is more than 40 times larger in goldens than in humans; in addition, goldens can remember thousands of odors and can associate them with the appropriate people, animals, places, and events. The ability to discriminate between odors makes goldens valuable for police narcotic and bomb squads.

Goldens also possess a highly developed sense of hearing, superior to that of humans. They hear a wider range of sounds, especially high-pitched frequencies, such as those emitted from a Galton whistle ("silent" dog whistle). Goldens hear sounds from a much greater distance than do humans. Their acute hearing is also important to their usefulness as hunting dogs.

Goldens' peripheral vision is much greater than that of humans; however, their eyes do not focus as sharply as do those of humans. As a result, their eyes are much more sensitive to motion, but they must rely more on smell and sound to interpret what they see.

As previously mentioned, goldens lack body sensitivity. This is important for hunting dogs that must run through thick brush and cold marshes in all types of weather.

Like other dogs, goldens possess other senses that we still do not understand completely. For example, they have an innate sense of navigation. We have all heard reports of dogs traveling hundreds of miles to return home to their masters.

From Puppy to Adult Dog

The most critical part of your golden puppy's life begins when you remove it from its littermates. From its seventh week on, your puppy begins to develop a new relationship with you. At this age your puppy is very curious and mischievous, and it lacks training. It must learn the rules of your home as well as to differentiate play from seriousness.

Even before you bring your puppy home, it will have tested its strength in mock fights with its littermates. This helps improve its motor skills. It will also have begun to test the rules through its interactions with its mother.

When you bring your puppy home, it will be exceptionally adaptable (physically and emotionally) and will learn readily. Therefore, do not hesitate to begin training it immediately.

By the time your puppy is 12 or 13 weeks old, it will be completely aware of both itself and your home. Its greatest joy will be to share discoveries with you. It will begin to investigate everything, primarily with its teeth, for at this time it begins to lose its baby teeth and get its permanent ones. Make sure you give your puppy enough toys to chew on. Remember that your puppy is still very impressionable, so treat it with care. Teach it the basic rules of your house, but be sure to be consistent and to control your emotions.

As your puppy reaches sexual maturity, it will enter a stage equivalent to human adolescence. At seven to ten months old it will almost reach its adult size. Its curiosity is now bold, assertive interest. It is much more comfortable with your lifestyle and feels it should be included in all your activities. By this time your golden should know what you expect of it and how it should behave. However, it will naturally try to challenge you in order to improve its rank. When this happens, do not lose your temper. Just teach your golden—calmly and firmly—that you are in charge. Doing so will lead your dog through its final stage of development.

Once your golden reaches maturity, it probably will not undergo any major behavioral changes (with the exception of mating urges). Your consistency and evenness of temper in training your dog should now pay off in many years of companionship with a loving, devoted, trustworthy golden retriever.

Encounters in the Outside World

It is important to familiarize your golden puppy with the ways of humans and other animals. Introducing your dog to the outside world while it is still very young will make vacations or other trips with your golden much more pleasant. Your dog will be much happier if it learns not to fear people or other dogs.

On occasion take your dog with you when you shop. Being exposed to strange places and people (as long as you accompany it) will help increase the puppy's confidence in itself and in you. Also take the dog on short auto trips. Gradually lengthen the trips until the puppy is used to traveling.

When you travel by car, keep your dog in a small cage to prevent it from getting in your way and to protect it from injury through sudden stops. If you cannot bring a cage, teach your dog to lie down on the back seat. Never let it ride with its head out the window, for it can get foreign matter in its eyes. When you leave your puppy in the car, always open the windows enough for proper ventilation, but not enough for the dog to jump out. Heat can build up in a car very rapidly, so always park in the shade. If you plan to be gone a long time, leave your dog at home.

In addition, walk your puppy (on a leash) in areas where you will encounter other people and dogs. If you like, let your golden play with other dogs. Restrain your puppy until the strange dog approaches it. If the two wag their tails and sniff each other's nose and tail, you may assume they like each other. Your golden puppy will almost always wag its tail. You can remove your puppy's leash if you wish, but remain nearby in case you are needed.

Your golden and a strange dog will almost always try to establish a ranking order. This may include playful frolicking in which one dog ends up lying on its back in a subordinate position. However, the dogs may fight if neither is willing to back down, so be prepared. If either dog tries to challenge the other by displaying a threatening posture or by growling, immediately remove your golden from the area.

How Your Dog Affects You

Recently, scientists have begun to study the psychological and behavioral responses of people to companion animals. Owning and caring for a pet is an effective means of reducing stress. It is also beneficial for the elderly as well as the physically and mentally handicapped. As the owner of a golden retriever, you will undoubtedly become emotionally attached to your dog. Do not think of this as strange, even if you find it embarrassing. Remember that it is only natural to become attached to a living being with whom you share a long-term emotional commitment—whether human or canine.

Sharing sport and adventure with your golden will mean sharing happiness, excitement, and friendship. Be assured that your dog will also experience these feelings and will often attempt to express its gratitude. Your golden will make you feel loved and appreciated. Whenever you return home, you will be greeted by a dog that is happy to see you and that missed you when you were gone.

Your golden will always love you for yourself. Your wealth or social and professional success are not important to it. It gives its love unquestionably and completely; what greater devotion can anyone demand?

Useful Addresses

Golden Retriever Club of America*
John W. McAssey
Route 7
Box 912
Talahassee, FL 32308

American Kennel Club
51 Madison Avenue
New York, NY 10038

Australian National Kennel Club
Royal Show Grounds
Ascot Vale
Victoria
Australia

Canadian Kennel Club
111 Eglington Avenue
Toronto 12, Ontario
Canada

Irish Kennel Club
41 Harcourt Street
Dublin 2
Ireland

The Kennel Club
1-4 Clargis Street
Picadilly
London W7Y 8AB
England

New Zealand Kennel Club
P.O. Box 523
Wellington
New Zealand

*These addresses may change as new officers are
elected. The latest listing can always be obtained
from the American Kennel Club.

Index

Active immunity 29 – 30
Adults 66
Afterbirth 49
Aggressiveness 64
Ailments 29 – 41
Air travel 23
Allergic reactions 34
Amniotic sac 47
Aujeszky's disease 25
Automobile travel 23

Babies and dogs 21 – 22
Basic training 50 – 60
Bathing 19
Bed 10
Bee stings 39
Beef 25
Behavior
    patterns 65
    problems 65
Birth of puppies 47
Boarding kennels 23
Body language 65
Bones, feeding of 14, 25, 26, 27
Breed
    characteristics 42 – 46
    history 61
    origin 61
    standard 42 – 46
Breeders 8 – 9
Breeding 42 – 49
    objectives 42
    poor practices 42, 65
Broken bones 39
Brushing 16 – 19

Cages 10, 51
Calcium 26
Canned dog food 26
Canine distemper 30
Canine hepatitis 30
Carbohydrates 25
Carrying a puppy 20
Cataracts 38
Chicken 25

Children and dogs 20
Chlorophyll tablets 23
Coat
    care of 16, 19
    color 45
Collars 12
Color 45
"Come" 52
Commercial dog foods 26
Communication
    body language 65
    vocal 65
Constipation 37
Cost
    of keeping 9
    of purchase 9

Demodedic mange 34
Diarrhea 29
Diethylcarbamazine 32
Digestive disorders 37
Dog house 11 – 12
Dog run 11
Dog shows 48 – 49
Dry dog food 26

Ear
    ailments 38
    care 20, 38
    shape 44
Eczema 34
Enteritis 37
Equipment 12 – 14
Esterus 22 – 23
External parasites 33
Eye
    care 20
    description of 44
    disorders 37

False pregnancy 38 – 39
Fat 25
Feeding
    areas 10, 11
    by age 27 – 28
    on vacation 24

pregnant dogs 47
puppies 47
schedules 27 – 28
Female dogs 8, 22 – 23
Fiber 25
Field trials 48 – 49
Flea sprays 13, 33
Fleas 33
Food
    cost of 9
    dish 12

Gait 45
Galton whistle 65
Gestation 47
Grooming 16
Guide dog training 59 – 60

Head shaking 38
Head shape 44
Hearing, sense of 65 – 66
Heartworm 32
Heeling 57
Hip dysplasia 9, 38
Housebreaking 51 – 52
Housing 10 – 12
Human-dog relationship 50, 62, 65
Hunter-dog relationship 62
Hurdles 60

Identification tags 12
Illness 29 – 41
Injured dogs, handling of 20, 40 – 41
Instincts 22, 62
Internal parasites 31 – 32

Jumping hurdles 58

Kennels 23

Laxatives 37
Leashes 13
Leptospirosis 30
Lice 33

Index

Lifting a dog   20
Lying down   58

Mange   34
Marking territory   62
Mating   46 – 47
Medication, administering
   40 – 41
Minerals   26
Mites   34
Motion sickness   23
Muzzles   13

Nail Care   19
Nose   44
Nursing a sick dog   40 – 41
Nutrition   25 – 28

Obedience training   56 – 60
Obedience trials   48
Origin of the breed   61
Outdoor run   11

Parainfluenza   30 – 31
Parvovirus   31
Passive immunity   29 – 30
Pedicures   19
Pedigree papers   8
Peripheral vision   66
Phosphorus   26
Poisoning   39
Pork   25
Pregnancy   46 – 47
   false   38
   prevention   22 – 23
Preventive medicine   29
Progressive retinal atrophy   37
Protein   25
Pulse, taking of   40
Puppies   8, 15 – 16, 66
   birth of   47
   buying of   8 – 9

care of   47 – 48
toys for   14

Rabies   31
Railroad transport   23
Ranking order   50
Rawhide bones   14
Reflecting tag   12
Relinquishing an object   58
Respiratory ailments   37
Retinal atrophy, progressive   37
Retrieving   58
Ringworm   37
Rocky Mountain spotted
   fever   33
Roughage   25
Roundworm   31, 48
Run, fenced   11

Sarcoptic mange   34
Seeing-eye dog   59 – 60
Semimoist dog food   26
Sense organs   65 – 66
Sexual differences   8
Shock   29
Show dogs, choosing of   8
"Sit"   55
Skin problems   34
Sleeping box   10
Smell, sense of   65 – 66
Social behavior   22
Spaying   8
Standard (AKC)   42 – 45
"Stay"   55 – 56
Stings, insect   39
Stool check   32
Symptoms, understanding   29

Tag   12
Tail
   shape   45
   wagging   65

Tapeworm   31 – 32
Teeth
   alignment   44
   care   19 – 20
Temperament
   description   45
   understanding   62
Temperature, taking of   40
Ticks   35
Tonsillitis   37
Touch, sense of   20, 66
Toys   14
Trace elements   26
Tracheobronchitis   30 – 31
Training   52 – 62
   cage   10
   problems   59
   puppies   51
   rules of   50 – 51
Travel   23 – 24
Trichiasis   38
Tweezers   13, 33

Umbilical cord   47

Vacations   23 – 24
Vaccination   29 – 30
   schedule   31
Vision, peripheral   66
Vitamins   26
Vocal communication   65
Vomiting   29

Wasp stings   39
Water   26
Water bowl   12
Weight of an adult   45
Wet nursing   47 – 48
Whelping   47
   box   47
Worming   31 – 32

Perfect for Pet Owners!

PET OWNER'S MANUALS

72-80 pages, over 50 illustrations
(20-plus color photos), paperback.

AFRICAN GRAY PARROTS Wolter (3773-1)
BANTAMS Fritzsche (3687-5)
BEAGLES Vriends-Parent (3829-0)
BOXERS Kraupa-Tuskany (4036-8)
CANARIES Frisch (2614-4)
CATS Fritzsche (2421-4)
CHINCHILLAS Thiede (4037-6)
COCKATIELS Wolter (2889-9)
DACHSHUNDS Fiedelmeier (2888-0)
DOBERMAN PINSCHERS Gudas (2999-2)
DWARF RABBITS Wegler (3669-7)
FEEDING AND SHELTERING
   EUROPEAN BIRDS von Frisch (2858-9)
FERRETS Morton (2976-3)
GERBILS Gudas (3725-1)
GERMAN SHEPHERDS Antesberger (2982-8)
GOLDEN RETRIEVERS Sucher (3793-6)
GOLDFISH Ostrow (2975-5)
GUINEA PIGS Bielfeld (2629-2)
HAMSTERS Fritzsche (2422-2)
LABRADOR RETRIEVERS Kern (3792-8)
LIZARDS IN THE TERRARIUM Jes (3925-4)
LONG-HAIRED CATS Müller (2803-1)
LOVEBIRDS Vriends (3726-X)
MICE Bielfeld (2921-6)
MYNAS von Frisch (3688-3)
NONVENOMOUS SNAKES Trutnau (5632-9)
PARAKEETS Wolter (2423-0)
PARROTS Deimer (2630-6)
PONIES Kraupa-Tuskany (2856-2)
POODLES Ullmann & Ullmann (2812-0)
RABBITS Fritzsche (2615-2)
SCHNAUZERS Frye (3949-1)
SNAKES Griehl (2813-9)
SPANIELS Ullmann & Ullmann (2424-9)
TROPICAL FISH Braemer & Scheumann (2686-1)
TURTLES Wilkie (2631-4)
WATER PLANTS IN THE
   AQUARIUM Scheurmann (3926-2)
ZEBRA FINCHES Martin (3497-X)

NEW PET HANDBOOKS

Detailed profiles with 40 to 60 color photos.
144 pages, paperback.

NEW AQUARIUM HANDBOOK Scheurmann (3682-4)
NEW CAT HANDBOOK Müller (2922-4)
NEW DOG HANDBOOK Ullmann (2857-0)
NEW FINCH HANDBOOK Koepff (2859-7)
NEW PARAKEET HANDBOOK Birmelin & Wolter (2985-2)
NEW PARROT HANDBOOK Lantermann (3729-4)
NEW TERRIER HANDBOOK Kern (3951-3)

CAT FANCIER'S SERIES

Authoritative colorful guides (over 35 color photos).
72 pages, paperback.

BURMESE CATS Swift (2925-9)
LONGHAIR CATS Pond (2923-3)
SIAMESE CATS Dunnill (2924-0)

NEW PREMIUM SERIES

Comprehensive, lavishly illustrated in color.
136-176 pages (60 to 300 color photos), hardcover.

AQUARIUM FISH SURVIVAL MANUAL Ward (5686-8)
CAT CARE MANUAL Viner (5765-1)
DOG CARE MANUAL Alderton (5764-3)
GOLDFISH AND ORNAMENTAL CARP
   Penzes & Tolg (5634-5)
LABYRINTH FISH Pinter (5635-3)

FIRST AID FOR PETS

20 pages, hardbound with hanging chain and index tabs,
fully illustrated in color.

FIRST AID FOR YOUR CAT Frye (5827-5)
FIRST AID FOR YOUR DOG Frye (5828-3)

ISBN prefix: 0-8120

Order from your favorite
book or pet store

BARRON'S

Be Ready To Save Your Pet's Life

With These Expert Manuals From Barron's...

First Aid For Your Dog

By Fredric L. Frye, D.V.M., M.S.
In this clearly-written guide with instructive illustrations, color-coded index tabs quickly point you to vital first aid techniques such as how to: give a heart massage and artificial respiration • stop bleeding • treat frostbite, convulsions and much more. (5828-3)

First Aid For Your Cat

By Fredric L. Frye, D.V.M., M.S.
This fully-illustrated, clear guide uses color-coded index tabs to give you quick access to life-saving steps such as how to: restrain and lift an injured cat • give artificial respiration • apply splints and tourniquets • treat gagging, poisoning and much more. (5827-5)

Each Book: Hardboard with hanging chain and index tabs, 20 pp., $9.95, Can. $13.95

Books may be purchased at your bookstore, pet store or by mail from Barron's. Enclose check or money order for total amount plus sales tax where applicable and 10% for postage (minimum charge $1.50).

In Canada: 195 Allstate Parkway Markham, Ontario L3R 4T8

Barron's Educational Series, Inc.
250 Wireless Blvd.
Hauppauge, NY 11788